Meiktila 1945

The battle to liberate Burma

Campaign • 136

Meiktila 1945

The battle to liberate Burma

Edward M Young • Illustrated by Howard Gerrard

First published in Great Britain in 2004 by Osprey Publishing,
Midland House, West Way, Botley, Oxford OX2 0PH, UK
44-02 23rd St, Suite 219, Long Island City, NY 11101, USA
Email: info@ospreypublishing.com

Transferred to digital print on demand 2010

First published 2004
2nd impression 2009

Printed and bound by PrintOnDemand-Worldwide.com Peterborough, UK

A CIP catalog record for this book is available from the British Library

ISBN: 978 1 84176 698 0

Series Editor: Lee Johnson
Design by The Black Spot
Index by Alison Worthington
Maps by The Map Studio
3D bird's-eye views by The Black Spot
Battlescene artwork by Howard Gerrard
Originated by The Electronic Page Company, Cwmbran, UK

Editor's note

To avoid confusion between Allied and Japanese units in this volume, the names or designations of all Allied units are shown in
roman text and all Japanese units in *italic* text.

Acknowledgments

I would like to thank my sister, Katherine Young, who acted as my translator on a visit to Meiktila; Mr. Maurice Packer of the Indian
and Oriental Collection, the British Library, who tracked down maps of the battle area; the staff of the Photograph Archive at the
Imperial War Museum for their help finding the many photographs used in this volume; and Osamu Tagaya for sharing his extensive
knowledge of the Japanese military in World War II.

Artist's note

Readers may care to note that the original paintings from which the color plates in this book were prepared are available for
private sale. All reproduction copyright whatsoever is retained by the Publisher. Enquiries should be addressed to:

Howard Gerrard
11 Oaks Road
Tenterden
Kent
TN30 6RD
UK

The Publishers regret that they can enter into no correspondence upon this matter.

The Woodland Trust

Osprey Publishing is supporting the Woodland Trust, the UK's leading woodland conservation charity,
by funding the dedication of trees.

www.ospreypublishing.com

Key to military series symbols

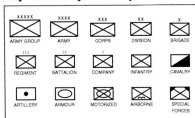

CONTENTS

ORIGINS OF THE CAMPAIGN   6

CHRONOLOGY   14

OPPOSING COMMANDERS   16

Japanese commanders • British commanders

OPPOSING PLANS   20

The Japanese plan • The British plan

OPPOSING FORCES   24

Japanese forces • British forces • Orders of battle

THE MEIKTILA CAMPAIGN   33

The advance to the Irrawaddy • The attack on Meiktila

The defense of Meiktila

AFTERMATH   87

THE BATTLEFIELD TODAY   92

SELECT BIBLIOGRAPHY   94

INDEX   95

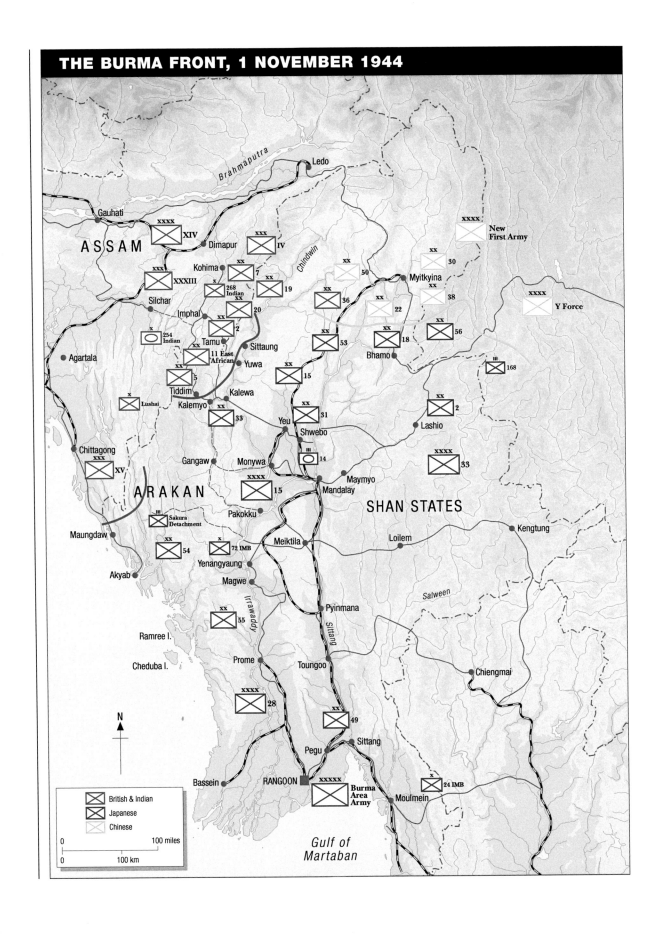

THE BURMA FRONT, 1 NOVEMBER 1944

Ledo

Brahmaputra

Gauhati

ASSAM

XXXX XIV

Dimapur

XXX IV

Chindwin

New First Army XXXX

Kohima

XXX XXXIII

Silchar

XX 7

XXX 50

Myitkyina

XX 30

X 268 Indian

XX 19

XX 20

XX 36

XX 22

XX 38

Y Force XXXX

Imphal

X 254 Indian

XX 2

Tamu

Sittaung

XX 53

XX 18

Bhamo

XX 56

Agartala

XX 11 East African

Yuwa

XX 15

III 168

XX 5

Tiddim

Kalewa

XX 31

Yeu

Shwebo

XX 2

Lashio

X Lushai

Kalemyo

XX 33

III 14

XXXX 33

Chittagong

XXX XV

Gangaw

Monywa

Maymyo

Mandalay

SHAN STATES

ARAKAN

XXXX 15

Pakokku

Kengtung

III Sakura Detachment

Maungdaw

XX 54

X 72 IMB

Meiktila

Loilem

Yenangyaung

Akyab

Magwe

Irrawaddy

Salween

Pyinmana

Ramree I.

XX 55

Cheduba I.

Prome

Toungoo

Chiengmai

Sittang

N

XXXX 28

XX 49

Sittang

Pegu

Bassein

RANGOON

XXXXX Burma Area Army

Moulmein

X 24 IMB

⊠ British & Indian
⊠ Japanese
⊠ Chinese

0 — 100 miles
0 — 100 km

Gulf of Martaban

ORIGINS OF THE CAMPAIGN

O n 22 June 1944, troops from the British 2nd Infantry Division, advancing down the Kohima–Imphal road from Kohima, linked up with Indian infantry from the 5th Indian Infantry Division coming out of Imphal. The Japanese siege of Imphal was broken. After three months of intense fighting, the ambitious Japanese advance into Assam would soon turn into a headlong retreat back to the Chindwin River and a return to Burma. The battle of Imphal was the turning point of the war in Burma. Victory at Imphal transformed the strategic situation in the Burma theater and presented an opportunity that had been considered impossible a few months before.

For the previous two years Allied strategy in Southeast Asia had been subject to a frustrating and often acrimonious debate between the American and the British high commands, reflecting clearly divergent strategic objectives. Central to American strategy for waging war against Japan was the need to keep China in the war. If China remained active in the war, the fighting would continue to absorb the Japanese armies that would otherwise be turned against the Americans in their march across the Pacific. In addition, China had the potential to serve as a base for an assault on Japan planned for later in the war. What China desperately needed were supplies to sustain her population, maintain and improve her armies, and support the American air effort against the Japanese. While the American Army Air Force had begun an airlift to China over the Hump route, the American Chiefs of Staff believed that the only effective way of providing supplies to China was to build a

Troops from 2nd British and 5th Indian Divisions meet on the Kohima–Imphal road, 22 June 1944. (IWM IND 3495)

7

land route across Assam and northern Burma to link up with the old Burma Road at the Burma-China border. The American objective was to clear the Japanese armies from northern Burma to protect the growing airfield complex in Assam, and ultimately to secure the land route to China.

British strategy for the war in Southeast Asia reflected a completely different strategic viewpoint from the Americans and a more pessimistic appreciation of the problems of terrain and logistics. The British high command was skeptical of China's value to the war effort, and did not believe that arming the Chinese would bring much benefit in the war against Japan. If China did need to be kept in the war, the more effective means of supply was to re-open the Burma Road by clearing the Japanese from central Burma and Rangoon. But Winston Churchill and the British Chiefs of Staff considered an overland advance to re-conquer Burma an appalling prospect. Churchill likened the idea of fighting the Japanese in the jungles of northern Burma to a man going into the water to fight a shark. The failed advance in the Arakan in early 1943 reinforced the view that the British and Indian forces available were by no means capable of fighting a jungle campaign against the Japanese. The terrain of Assam and northern Burma, where any campaign would have to be fought, is some of the worst in the world in which to conduct a military campaign, a series of jungle-covered mountain ranges with horrendous heat, torrential rains, and crippling diseases. The lack of a road and rail system through Assam and Burma capable of supporting a modern army in the strength necessary to defeat the Japanese presented logistical problems that seemed insurmountable. The British looked beyond Burma to their colonies in Malaya and Singapore, and to the Dutch East Indies, the source of much of Japan's oil, as more important strategic objectives. If Burma had to be retaken, it would be far better to achieve this via a sea-borne invasion rather than an overland advance. Even better, in the view of some, would be to by-pass Burma altogether to attack Malaya or the Dutch East Indies. More critically, with the defeat of Germany given priority, Britain had precious few resources left to devote to a major campaign in Southeast Asia prior to Germany's defeat. Burma would, perforce, be lowest on the list of priorities. As a result of these views, the British Chiefs of Staff's enthusiasm for the American proposals was lukewarm at best.

Lieutenant-General William Slim, appointed commander of the 14th Army in the fall of 1943, did not agree with the conventional wisdom that an overland advance to retake Burma was, for all practical purposes, impossible. Slim recognized full well the logistical problems he faced. The campaign in Burma would be a struggle with supply and terrain just as much as a battle with the enemy, but he believed these problems were not insurmountable. Having retreated out of Burma in 1942, Slim knew that the central plain of Burma was open country well suited to tanks and combined arms warfare, where the 14th Army, even with its few resources, would still be superior to the Japanese armies facing them. If he could get a force through the northern mountain jungles and into the central plain, he could bring this superiority to bear and defeat the Japanese in a decisive battle. If he could find some way of weakening the Japanese army before attempting an overland advance, the forces required to defeat the Japanese in the central plains could be reduced, and be successfully

Jeeps bringing up supplies on the Imphal–Tiddim road. During the monsoon the condition of these tracks was appalling. (IWM IND 3958)

supported with the limited road and rail system available from India through Assam. While wrestling with these problems, Slim devoted his energy and his considerable leadership skills to rebuilding his army into a fighting force capable of soundly defeating the Japanese.

At the "Quadrant' Conference in August 1943, the Allies did work out a compromise strategy for Burma and the formation of a separate South-East Asia Command under Admiral Lord Louis Mountbatten as Supreme Allied Commander. The Americans and the British Chiefs of Staff agreed on a limited advance during the 1943/44 dry season in the Arakan and northern Burma by British forces and Chinese forces under General Joseph Stillwell in the Northern Combat Area Command (N.C.A.C.), combined with a second, and larger, Chindit operation under Major-General Orde Wingate, to ensure the security of the American airfields and to lay a foundation for later operations to restore land communications with China. It was hoped this offensive would be combined with sea-borne operations to keep maximum pressure on the Japanese. In the event, the landing craft and support forces necessary for sea-borne attacks never materialized, while a new and powerful Japanese initiative completely changed the face of the battle for northern Burma.

Operation "U-Go"

In the aftermath of their victorious march through Asia and the Pacific, the Japanese strategy was to create a defensive barrier around their newly conquered territories and hold this barrier against any Allied attack, inflicting such heavy casualties that the Allies would cease fighting. Burma was the Japanese barrier protecting Southeast Asia and its vital oil and mineral resources. The Japanese *Southern Army*, which had responsibility for all Imperial Japanese Army operations in Southeast Asia and the Southwest Pacific, had assigned responsibility for the defense of Burma to *Burma Area Army*, whose task it was to defeat any Allied attempt to re-take Burma as well as to disrupt communications between India and China. Ironically, the first

Where even jeeps could not get through, men and mules took over. Here a reserve company of 5th Indian Division carries supplies forward to the front line. (IWM IND 4061)

Chindit expedition into Burma in 1943 caused the Japanese command in Burma to reconsider their defensive strategy. Wingate and his Chindits had shown that a strong force could cross the mountains between India and Burma and cross the Chindwin River with relative ease. Inspired by Wingate's operation, Lieutenant-General Mutaguchi Renya, commander of the *15th Army* in Burma, argued forcefully to the *Burma Area Army* commander, Lieutenant-General Kawabe Masakazu, that if the Japanese wanted to forestall and defeat a British offensive into Burma, then they must capture Imphal, the base for any offensive. After careful study by *Burma Area Army* and *Southern Army*, in January 1944 the Japanese *Imperial General Headquarters* gave approval for Operation "U-Go", the capture of Imphal and an advance into Assam, to be launched in the 1944 dry season. To tie down British forces in the Arakan, "U-Go" would be preceded by Operation "Ha-Go", an attack on the Akyab front.

Mutaguchi began his campaign against Imphal during the first week of March, sending two of *15th Army's* divisions to attack and isolate Imphal, while the third attacked Kohima to cut the British lines of communication back to the railhead at Dimapur. With an appalling disregard for the logistical needs of his divisions, Mutaguchi expected the campaign to take three weeks, and promised his soldiers that they would find all the supplies they needed in the British dumps at Imphal. The result was an unmitigated disaster, the worst defeat the Japanese army ever experienced. By the end of the battle, the Japanese had suffered over 60,000 casualties with severe losses in guns and equipment. The remnants of *15th Army* that staggered back to the Chindwin and Burma were badly weakened by disease, malnutrition, and combat losses. Slim and his corps and division commanders had conducted a masterful defensive campaign. The British and Indian troops at Imphal and Kohima had fought superbly well, benefiting from better training, better morale, and better supplies. Air transport had kept up a steady flow of supplies and reinforcements to Imphal, proving that the 14th Army was not completely tied to a road system, as many had supposed.

The magnitude of the Japanese defeat became apparent as British and Indian troops pushed out of Imphal in pursuit of the retreating Japanese forces. All along the tracks and trails lay evidence of the disaster, dead and dying soldiers, abandoned trucks and tanks, and abandoned guns; sights few had seen in the campaign before. As he read the intelligence reports, Slim realized that the Japanese had given him the opportunity he had hoped for. The extent of Japanese losses meant that it would take time for *Burma Area Army* to regroup and prepare a defense. If 14th Army could keep the pressure on the retreating Japanese, Slim could push a force across the Chindwin River and deep into the central plain before the Japanese had time to recover. There he could engage the Japanese Army with the forces he had available and, in its weakened state, destroy it. If the Japanese Army in Burma could be destroyed in the central plain, then all of lower Burma would be open, and 14th Army could continue on to capture Rangoon. With this ambitious goal in mind, Slim immediately set about planning an offensive to capture Mandalay and Rangoon, and proposed this plan to Mountbatten.

In early June the Combined Chiefs of Staff had given Mountbatten a new directive for operations in Burma that limited his objectives to protecting the "Hump" air link and to exploiting the opportunity for building an overland route to China. Mountbatten now recognized that the strategic situation had moved well beyond this limited mission. With the failure of the Japanese offensive into Assam, the air link needed less protection, and the best way to create the overland route to China was to make a general advance into central Burma, as Slim was proposing. Working with the commanders of his air, land, and sea forces, Mountbatten developed a more ambitious plan that he submitted to the British Chiefs of Staff in August. Stressing the need to exploit the Japanese defeat at Imphal, Mountbatten proposed two operations, "Capital" and "Dracula". In "Capital", Mountbatten proposed an advance by 14th Army and Chinese forces in the N.C.A.C. to the line Pakokku–Mandalay–Lashio, with 14th Army advancing to capture Mandalay, thereby gaining control of the central plain. "Dracula" envisioned a combined airborne and amphibious assault on Rangoon, which would then push north to link up with 14th Army, liberating all of Burma. While Mountbatten believed that South-East Asia Command could accomplish Operation "Capital" with the forces available in the theater, Operation "Dracula", as proposed, would require troops and shipping released from Europe. In either case, Mountbatten was now committing South-East Asia Command to the re-conquest of Burma. At the "Octagon" Conference in September, the Combined Chiefs of Staff, the Prime Minister, and President Roosevelt gave their approval to Mountbatten's proposal.

Imphal forced the Japanese to redraw their plans for operations in Burma as well. The losses *Burma Area Army* had suffered could not be fully made good given pressures across the Pacific, where the Americans were advancing across a broad front. Nor could *Burma Area Army* be expected to defend Burma and disrupt communications between India and China with the remaining forces it had available. *Imperial General Headquarters* therefore instructed *Burma Area Army* to put priority on defending southern Burma in order to protect *Southern Army's* western flank. To carry out this new directive, *Imperial General Headquarters* ordered a change in the higher command in Burma. In an unprecedented move, on 30 August 1944, Lieutenant-General Kimura Hyotaro replaced Lieutenant-General

Jemmadar Gopal Singh,
4th Jammu and Kashmir Infantry,
points out Japanese positions
to Captain Hassan Khan from
the summit of Kennedy Peak.
(IWM IND 4070)

Kawabe as commander of *Burma Area Army*, while the commander of *54th Division*, Lieutenant-General Katamura Shihachi, replaced Lieutenant-General Mutaguchi as commander of *15th Army*.

In anticipation of "Capital", Slim had kept his forces pushing hard against the retreating Japanese despite the onset of the monsoon, which turned small streams into rushing torrents and jungle tracks into rivers of mud. By early August the Imphal plain had been cleared of all Japanese forces. Slim ordered an advance across a broad front to give the Japanese no time to regroup. Under the command of XXXIII Corps, 14th Army divisions fought their way down the Tamu and Tiddim roads against Japanese rearguards, which even in their weakened state fought desperately to cover their retreat. 14th Army's objective was the Chindwin River, where the advance into central Burma would begin. On 14 November the town of Kalemyo was found abandoned and, on 2 December, troops of the 11th East African Division captured Kalewa on the Chindwin River. Slim wasted no time, putting a force across the Chindwin opposite Kalewa during the night of 3 December. In preparation for crossing the Chindwin, Slim had instructed 19th Division of IV Corps to move forward and cross the river further north opposite Sittaung, then advance on Pinlebu and Pinbon. Under its aggressive commander, Major-General "Pete" Rees, 19th Division moved swiftly across country, capturing Pinlebu on 14 December. Two days later it linked up with the British 36th Division, working with the Chinese forces, linking 14th Army's front with the N.C.A.C. front for the first time.

The ease and speed with which the Chindwin was crossed and 19th Division reached Pinlebu raised doubts in Slim's mind about Japanese intentions. Slim's orders under Operation "Capital" were to advance into central Burma and capture Mandalay, but he realized that the destruction of the Japanese Army in Burma was more important than the capture of any town. His own goal was to force the Japanese Army into a second decisive battle and destroy it. Slim was convinced that Kimura would defend Mandalay and the approaches to southern Burma by fighting in the Shwebo plain, the area to the south of Shwebo enclosed by the Irrawaddy

River to the east and south, and the Chindwin to the west. Slim planned to send his two Corps, with five divisions, three infantry brigades, and two tank brigades, on a broad sweep down to this plain, with IV Corps on the left flank following the Irrawaddy River and XXXIII Corps on the right, putting pressure on the Japanese from all sides. In the Shwebo plain he would engage the Japanese, with their backs to the Irrawaddy, in a combined arms attack using his tanks and infantry in the open country, with close air support, to annihilate them.

The intelligence coming to Slim now indicated that the Japanese were not preparing to fight in the Shwebo plain, but were in headlong retreat. On 1 December, Kimura had in fact ordered all units to retreat back across the Irrawaddy. Slim realized he had made a mistake and had completely misjudged Kimura's intentions. Unlike his predecessors, Kimura demonstrated a far greater realism in his appreciation of the situation he faced, and a willingness to be more flexible in his response. Instead of fighting 14th Army on the approaches to Mandalay with the Irrawaddy at his back, as Slim had expected him to do, Kimura had retreated and would now force 14th Army to cross the Irrawaddy to attack him, a far more difficult proposition. Slim realized he had to come up with a new plan, one that would still achieve his goal of forcing the Japanese into a decisive battle on terms that would still give 14th Army the advantage.

CHRONOLOGY

1944

15 March Japanese 15th Army launches operation "U-Go".

29 March Japanese forces cut the Kohima–Imphal road, surrounding Imphal.

22 June Troops from the 2nd Infantry Division, advancing from Kohima, make contact with troops of the 5th Indian Infantry Division coming up from Imphal. The Japanese siege of Imphal is broken.

4 July *Southern Area Army* commander approves *Burma Area Army*'s recommendation to abandon Imphal offensive and withdraw back to Burma.

16 September Combined Chiefs of Staff approve Operation "Capital", the overland advance into Burma.

17 December General Slim proposes Operation "Extended Capital".

20–21 December IV Corps and XXXIII Corps begin implementation of "Extended Capital".

19–22 December 7th Indian Infantry Division and 28th East African Brigade begin moving down the Myittha Valley.

22–26 December XXXIII Corps moves 2nd Infantry Division and 20th Indian Infantry Division across the Chindwin to join the advance toward the Irrawaddy.

1945

7 January 19th Indian Infantry Division captures Thabeikkyin on the east bank of the Irrawaddy River.

9 January 2nd Infantry Division captures Shwebo.

10 January 7th Division captures Gangaw.

11 January 19th Indian Infantry Division establishes a second bridgehead across the Irrawaddy River at Kyaukmyaung.

22 January 20th Indian Infantry Division captures Monywa.

31 January 2nd Infantry Division begins attack on Sagaing.

10 February 7th Division captures Kanhla. Slim orders general advance by 14th Army.

12 February 20th Division begins crossing the Irrawaddy River opposite Myinmu.

14 February 7th Division begins crossing the Irrawaddy River at Nyaungu. By nightfall three battalions are established in the bridgehead.

21 February 17th Division begins the advance on Meiktila, 82 miles (132km) away. A column of 3,000 vehicles leaves the bridgehead with 48th Brigade in the lead.

22 February 5th (Probyn's) Horse and 6/7 Rajputs encounter fanatical Japanese resistance at the village of Oyin, which is captured around midday. To the east, 19th Division links up around Kyaukmyaung and begins driving south towards Mandalay.

24 February 48th Brigade captures Taungtha in the afternoon; 63rd Brigade links up shortly thereafter. That night, 2nd Division begins crossing the Irrawaddy to the east of 20th Division's bridgehead, opposite Ngazun.

26 February 63rd Brigade captures Mahlaing in the morning, while a force of tanks and infantry make a wide sweep to the left and capture Thabutkon airfield, 13 miles (21km) from Meiktila.

27 February 99th Brigade begins fly-in to Thabutkon.

28 February Cowan launches the attack on Meiktila.

1 March 48th, 63rd, and 255th Tank Brigades push into the town against fierce opposition. Slim and Messervy visit Meiktila to confer with Cowan and view the fighting.

3 March After bitter fighting, the last Japanese opposition is cleared from Meiktila.

4 March 99th Brigade abandons Thabutkon airfield and moves to the airfield at Meiktila, which starts operations the next day. 99th Brigade assumes responsibility for defending Meiktila.

7–14 March Cowan sends strong armored columns on sweeps in all directions, breaking up concentrations of Japanese troops.

15 March Japanese forces launch a series of attacks against the airfield at Meiktila. Heavy artillery fire disrupts the air landings.

17 March 63rd Brigade sends two columns with tanks from 5th (Probyn's) Horse on sweeps around the Myindawgan area, bounded by the Meiktila–Yegyo railroad and the Meiktila–Pindale road, to clear out Japanese artillery.

18 March 99th Brigade undertakes sweeps of other areas with tanks from 9th (Royal Deccan) Horse. The force encounters very heavy gunfire, losing four tanks.

20 March 19th Division captures Fort Dufferin, and the Japanese abandon Mandalay.

21 March 9th (Royal Deccan) Horse and infantry attack a group of villages around Shwepadaing, encountering strong Japanese resistance despite air and artillery strikes.

22 March 7th Division captures Myingyan, opening the road to Meiktila. The attack around Shwepadaing resumes with heavy casualties. At the end of the day the force withdraws. That same day 99th Brigade sends a force to clear villages around Nyaungbintha. That night a large Japanese force makes a suicidal attack on 48th Brigade perimeter leaving 195 dead.

23 March 20th Division, moving down from Wundwin, makes contact with 17th Division around Meiktila.

24 March 20th Division force links up with 19th Division pushing south from Mandalay.

27–29 March Concluding effort by the Japanese to retake Meiktila. 63rd Brigade with tanks makes determined effort to clear out strong Japanese positions around Lake Myindawgan area.

30 March Slim starts the drive on Rangoon by IV Corps and XXXIII Corps. 17th Division starts moving on Pyawbwe in a planned envelopment of the town by the Division's three brigades with 255th Indian Tank Brigade in support.

10 April After surrounding Pyawbwe, 17th Division destroys the remaining garrison, and with it the *33rd Army*.

12 April 7th Division captures Kyaukpadaung on the Irrawaddy River, leading XXXIII Corps' advance down the Irrawaddy toward Rangoon.

20 April XXXIII Corps captures Magwe, while IV Corps divisions clear Pyinmana and Lewe.

25 April 5th Division captures Toungoo.

1 May 17th Division captures Pegu, 50 miles (81km) from Rangoon, but torrential rains prevent a move further south. Operation "Dracula", the capture of Rangoon, begins that morning with a paratroop attack on Elephant Point. The Japanese abandon Rangoon and retreat east.

3 May Allied forces occupy Rangoon.

OPPOSING COMMANDERS

JAPANESE COMMANDERS

Field Marshal Count Terauchi Hisaichi had commanded *Southern Army* since its activation in November 1941. *Southern Army* had responsibility for all Japanese Army operations in Southeast Asia and the Southwest Pacific. The son of a former Prime Minister, Terauchi had joined the Army in 1900 as a 2nd Lieutenant in the Infantry. He rose to command a division and, after appointment to General in 1935, served as War Minister for a brief period. In 1937 Terauchi was commander of the North China Area Army during the initial months of the Sino-Japanese War. He returned to Tokyo to serve as a Military Councilor until his appointment to command *Southern Army*. Having approved Operation "U-Go", he retained his command after the Operation's failure, unlike his subordinates.

    Lieutenant-General Kimura Hyotaro, who replaced Lieutenant-General Kawabe Masakazu as commander of *Burma Area Army*, began his Army career in 1908 as a lieutenant of artillery. He spent 20 years in the artillery branch, alternating unit commands with staff positions as he moved up the officer ranks. In the early 1930s Kimura was assigned to the War Ministry, where he remained for the next ten years. He became a Major-General in 1936, and served as Vice Minister of War from 1941–43 in General Tojo's cabinet. In 1944 he became Head of the Ordinance Administration at Imperial General Headquarters. Despite his lack of operational experience, he had a reputation as one of the smartest generals in the Japanese Army.

Lieutenant-General Kimura Hyotaro, *Burma Area Army* commander. (IWM SE 6873)

FAR, LEFT **Lieutenant-General Katamura Shihachi, *15th Army*.** (IWM AL5309)

LEFT **Lieutenant-General Honda Masaki, *33rd Army*.** (IWM AL5309)

The commanders of the three armies under *Burma Area Army's* control were all experienced, professional soldiers. **Lieutenant-General Katamura Shihachi** commanded *15th Army*. Katamura had been commander of the *54th Division*, which arrived in Burma in January 1944. After fighting on the Arakan front for some eight months through Operation "Ha-Go", Katamura was promoted to replace Lieutenant-General Mutaguchi as commander of *15th Army* in September 1944. A career infantry officer, **Lieutenant-General Honda Masaki** assumed command of *33rd Army* when it was activated in April 1944. Honda had served in China as Chief of Staff to the China Expeditionary Force and Manchuria as a division and Army commander, and was serving in a senior staff position in Tokyo when ordered to Burma. **Lieutenant-General Sakurai Shozo**, *28th Army* commander, had commanded the *33rd Division* in China and in the invasion of Burma in 1942. He became commander of *28th Army* at its activation in January 1944 and led it through Operation "Ha-Go" in the Arakan.

Lieutenant-General Sakurai Shozo, *28th Army*. (IWM AL 5309)

BRITISH COMMANDERS

Admiral Lord Louis Mountbatten, Supreme Allied Commander, South-East Asia Command, had responsibility for all operations in a theater stretching from Burma to the Dutch East Indies. To direct all land operations in Burma, the Allies agreed to the appointment of a Commander-in-Chief, Allied Land Forces, South-East Asia, under Mountbatten, to command all American, Chinese, and British land forces. In November 1944, **Lieutenant-General Sir Oliver Leese**, who had commanded the British 8th Army in Italy, arrived in India to take up this new command.

In command of 14th Army, South-East Asia Command's principle force, was **Lieutenant-General Sir William Slim**, one of the greatest generals of World War II. Slim had fought in the Middle East in World

Admiral Lord Louis Mountbatten, General Sir William Slim, and General Sir Oliver Leese. (IWM IND 4691)

War I, and had joined the Indian Army after the war to become a professional soldier, serving for many years with the Gurkhas. He commanded an Indian brigade in Eritrea, and was commanding a division in Iraq when he was appointed commander of the hurriedly organized Burma Corps in March 1942. He led the retreat out of Burma, preventing a defeat from turning into a disaster, and was then promoted to command XV Corps in India. He assumed command of 14th Army in October 1943. Slim was instrumental in the transformation of a defeated and completely demoralized force into a confident, well trained, and formidable army – one of the most remarkable transformations in military history. With his exceptional powers of leadership, Slim restored his army's morale and gave it a mission: the destruction of the Japanese Army in Burma. Slim had a firm grasp of logistics, which, with terrain, was the dominant factor in the Burma campaign. As a defensive general, he orchestrated the successful defense of Imphal; the battle for Meiktila would demonstrate his brilliance in the attack.

Slim was blessed with exceptionally capable subordinates. Like their Japanese counterparts, his corps and division commanders were all highly experienced professional soldiers, each with several years of active wartime service behind them. In command of IV Corps, which bore the brunt of the Meiktila battle, was **Lieutenant-General Sir Frank Messervy**, another career Indian Army officer. Messervy had spent two years fighting in the Western Desert, commanding the 4th Indian Infantry Division and the 7th Armored Division, and at one point escaping on foot through German lines. He returned to India in 1943 to command the 43rd Indian Armored Division, and then served as Director of Armored Vehicles, before taking command of 7th Indian Infantry Division, which he led through the battles in the Arakan and Imphal and Kohima. In October 1944 he was promoted to the command of IV Corps, and led it through to the end of the Burma campaign.

Lieutenant-General Sir Frank Messervy, IV Corps. (IWM SE 3054)

Major-General D.T. Cowan (center), 17th Indian Division. (IWM IND 4689)

Major-General Geoffrey Evans, 7th Indian Division. (IWM SE 3185)

Major-General Geoffrey Evans assumed command of 7th Indian Infantry Division following Messervy's promotion to command of IV Corps. An officer in the British Army, Evans began the war as a Captain and by 1944 was a Major-General. He had served in Eritrea and North Africa as a brigade major then battalion commander and had been posted to India in 1942 as commandant of the Indian Army staff college at Quetta. In 1943 he left to serve on the staff of IV Corps. He commanded a brigade in 5th Indian Infantry Division during the battles in the Arakan fighting off the Japanese "Ha-Go" offensive, then held command of another brigade after the division was airlifted to fight at Imphal. He took command of the division after the siege was lifted, and lead it in pursuit of the retreating Japanese.

Like Bill Slim, **Major-General D.T. "Punch" Cowan**, commander of 17th Indian Infantry Division, had fought in World War I and then joined the Indian Army. Cowan had served with Slim in the 6th Gurkha Rifles during the interwar years. He was appointed commander of 17th Division in the midst of the retreat from Burma in 1942, winning the DSO for his outstanding leadership. He was to lead the division throughout the Burma campaign, from defeat to victory, inspiring his troops during the dark days of the retreat, the intense fighting around Imphal, and the brilliant capture and defense of Meiktila.

Slim's second corps, XXXIII Corps, was under the command of **Lieutenant-General Sir Montague Stopford**, a British Army officer who had commanded the Corps through the Imphal battles. **Major-General C.G.G. Nicholson** commanded 2nd Infantry Division. Trained as an artillery officer, Nicholson had spent most of the war with armored divisions, and had commanded the 44th Indian Armored Division prior to taking command of 2nd Infantry Division at the end of 1944. **Major-General T.W. "Pete" Rees**, a diminutive Welshman and career Indian Army officer, commanded 19th Indian Infantry Division. Renowned for his excellent leadership and intensity, Rees lead his division from the front. **Major-General Douglas Gracy** had taken command of 20th Indian Infantry Division soon after its formation in 1942. Like Slim and Cowan, Gracy had fought in World War I and spent the interwar years in the Indian Army serving with the Gurkhas. He had led his division through the fighting at Imphal and in the advance to the Chindwin.

OPPOSING PLANS

THE JAPANESE PLAN

In defending southern Burma, Kimura needed to ensure that *Burma Area Army* retained control of the oil fields around Yenangyaung and the rice growing areas of the Irrawaddy delta to sustain his armies. His objective was to hold a line running from Lashio to Mandalay, the east bank of the Irrawaddy running from Mandalay to the area around Yenangyaung, and from Yenangyaung to Ramree Island on the Burma coast. Kimura had three armies, *15th, 28th,* and *33rd,* comprising eight divisions, one independent mixed brigade, and one tank regiment to defend this line. In addition he had two divisions and one independent mixed brigade in reserve, as well as line of communications troops and two divisions of the Indian National Army, of doubtful fighting value. All his divisions were under strength, and *15th Army* had lost much of its transport and artillery in the Imphal battles. Kimura realized that he could not put this weakened force against 14th Army in the Shwebo plain. While he could make up some of his troop losses by drawing on replacements from other forces in Southeast Asia, his losses in material would be much harder, if not impossible, to replace. In November *Imperial Japanese Headquarters* informed Kimura that he was effectively on his own and could expect no more reinforcements from Japan. This knowledge put a premium on using the Irrawaddy River as a barrier in his defense of southern Burma. After intense debate Kimura's staff all

Toward the end of October advance units of 14th Army had reached Tiddim, less than 50 miles from the Chindwin River and Burma's central plain. A 5th Indian Division soldier looks down on the town. (IWM IND 3999).

A Model 96 150mm howitzer abandoned near Tiddim. By this stage of the war, *Burma Area Army* could not make good the losses of men and equipment at Imphal. (IWM IND 3950)

agreed that the correct course was to defend from the east bank of the Irrawaddy, thereby forcing 14th Army to make an opposed river crossing, one of the most difficult of all military operations. This plan would also draw 14th Army that much farther from its sources of supply, while bringing the Japanese forces that much closer to their own supplies, a critical factor given Allied air superiority.

Kimura arrayed his armies along the line he intended to defend. He ordered *33rd Army*, with *18th* and *56th Divisions*, plus one regiment from *49th Division*, to hold the area from Lashio to Mandalay. *15th Army*, with *15th*, *31st*, and *33rd Divisions*, and *53rd Division* in reserve, would defend the east bank of the Irrawaddy from Mandalay to the area opposite Pakokku. *28th Army*, with *54th* and *55th Divisions* and the *72 Independent Mixed Brigade*, plus one regiment from *49th Division*, would be responsible for defending the area around the Yenangyaung oil fields to the Arakan, and the Irrawaddy delta area. In reserve, Kimura had *2nd Division*, the remaining units of *49th Division*, and *24th Independent Mixed Brigade*.

Kimura expected that 14th Army's objective would be to capture Mandalay. As the ancient capital of Burma, Mandalay had tremendous prestige value. The Burmese would interpret the loss of Mandalay as losing control of all Burma. In addition, if Mandalay was captured, it would sever the links between *15th Army* and *33rd Army*, and end any chance of breaking communications between India and China, still one of *Burma Area Army's* assigned tasks. For these reasons Kimura was determined to hold it. Here Kimura failed to appreciate that Slim's goal was not territory, but the destruction of Kimura's armies. The focus of Kimura's defensive plan remained tied to Mandalay. He fully expected 14th Army to cross the Irrawaddy to capture Mandalay, and believed that 14th Army would likely establish a bridgehead across the Irrawaddy north of Mandalay, and a second bridgehead to the southwest, to envelop the city from two directions. Kimura believed that once 14th Army had committed itself, he would be able to counterattack and hold the east bank of the Irrawaddy using the divisions of *15th Army*, and by bringing in *18th Division* and *49th Division* as reinforcements. If he could hold until the onset of the monsoon, then 14th Army's lines of communication would be badly stretched. British forces would likely be unable to advance any farther south, and without supplies, would be more vulnerable to further counterattacks, possibly being forced back to the Chindwin. He therefore instructed his armies to defend their assigned sectors, but be prepared to send reinforcements to the battles around Mandalay. He kept *49th Division* to the south in order to deploy it as the situation demanded.

In reviewing the strategic situation facing them, the *Burma Area Army* and *15th Army* staff had given some consideration to the defense of the town of Meiktila, the administrative and lines of communication center for *15th* and *33rd Armies* that lay some 80 miles (129km) from the Irrawaddy River. Surrounded by four airfields, Meiktila sat astride the main road from Rangoon to Mandalay and was some ten miles (16km) from the main Rangoon–Mandalay rail line. Here were the supply dumps and administrative support centers for the armies fighting further north. The town was lightly defended, mainly by two airfield defense battalions and an anti-aircraft battalion covering the main airfields. The majority of the approximately 4,000 Japanese troops in the town were from transport or supply units, or casualties recuperating at local hospitals. Some staff officers were concerned that the British might attempt to capture Meiktila, but the majority believed that the British would not be able to mount more than a nuisance raid against the town because they would need all their resources to take Mandalay. The staff concluded that the airfield defense units already in Meiktila could deal with a raid, and as the majority view prevailed, nothing more was done to prepare the town's defense.

THE BRITISH PLAN

Slim, too, was looking at Meiktila. As he cast about for a new plan that would force the Japanese to give battle, Slim and his staff realized that if 14th Army could capture Meiktila, they would have a strangle-hold on Kimura's supplies and lines of communications to his armies fighting further north. Kimura would have no choice but to respond to free his supply lines. More critically, if Slim could force Kimura to commit his forces to battle around Mandalay and then seize Meiktila by surprise when the Japanese armies were already heavily engaged, Kimura would have to fight two battles simultaneously, and commit all the forces he had in central Burma. This would bring on the decisive battle Slim wanted, and that he was confident he could win.

Slim's new plan required deception, surprise, and speed. To succeed he would have to convince Kimura that 14th Army's entire strength was bent towards Mandalay, conceal a force and push it to Meiktila before Kimura could ascertain his intentions, and capture the town before Kimura could react. He decided to have XXXIII Corps, with three divisions and one tank brigade, advance on a broad front toward the Irrawaddy River, as 14th Army had started to do, then cross the river north

In the coming battle Slim could count on having air superiority to protect his vital transport aircraft and support his infantry. RAF ground crew arm rocket-firing Hurricane Mk. IVs of No. 20 Squadron, which went into action for the first time in January 1945. (IWM CI 992)

and west of Mandalay to draw in Kimura's divisions for the defense of the city. At the same time he would send IV Corps, with two divisions an infantry brigade and his second tank brigade, far to the west to move down the valley of the Myittha River in complete secrecy. IV Corps would then advance toward Pakokku, and cross the Irrawaddy nearby to establish a bridgehead. Without pausing to consolidate IV Corps would then send a strong armored force with a large contingent of mechanized infantry to seize Meiktila. Slim intended IV Corps to act as an anvil with XXXIII Corps as the hammer, driving south from Mandalay.

The logistical challenges were formidable. Slim was proposing to send two divisions of troops and a brigade of tanks, in all several thousand vehicles, down a valley of several hundred miles over little more than a dirt track. IV Corps would have to build its own road as it went. All of this would have to be accomplished without the Japanese becoming aware of what was happening. IV Corps would have to break out of the valley and advance to the Irrawaddy River, where the Japanese were sure to notice such a large force. His divisions would then have to make an opposed river crossing, with inadequate equipment, establish a firm bridgehead, and push the Meiktila assault force across in record time. Once out of the bridgehead, the assault force would be entirely dependent on air supply until one of the airfields around Meiktila could be captured. At the same time, Slim would have to ensure a steady flow of supplies to XXXIII Corps' divisions fighting separate but equally intense battles miles apart. This would stretch his supply lines to their limit, and make all of 14th Army critically dependent on air transport.

Deception would play a prominent role in the lead-up to the battle. Slim had to convince Kimura that he was aiming for Mandalay, but at the same time cause maximum confusion to keep the Japanese constantly off-guard. He planned to use multiple crossings of the Irrawaddy, at different points and at different times, with feints at other points to create confusion. This would require careful coordination, because there was not enough equipment to support many crossings. Slim also needed the Chinese forces in the N.C.A.C. and British forces in the Arakan to keep up the pressure on the Japanese so that Kimura would not be able to draw reinforcements from these fronts.

Slim allocated to XXXIII Corps the divisions that were either east of the Chindwin or preparing to cross it. These were the 2nd, 19th, and 20th Divisions, the 268th Indian Infantry Brigade, and the 254th Indian Tank Brigade. Although 19th Division was part of IV Corps, it was the farthest to the east and it made little sense to have the division move back to rejoin IV Corps in its march down the Myittha Valley. This transfer had the added benefit that the Japanese identified 19th Division with IV Corps, which would aid in the deception plan. To IV Corps, Slim allocated 7th Division, 17th Division (then resting in India), 28th East African Brigade, the Lushai Brigade, and 255th Indian Tank Brigade.

On 17 December 1944, Slim advised Lieutenant-General Sir Oliver Leese, commander of Allied Land Forces South East Asia, of his new plan. The next day Slim met with his two Corps commanders, Lieutenant-General Sir Frank Messervy, commander of IV Corps, and Lieutenant-General Sir Montague Stopford, commander of XXXIII Corps, and briefed them on Operation 'Extended Capital', Slim's revised plan. Wasting no time, Slim gave the two commanders verbal orders to get started.

OPPOSING FORCES

JAPANESE FORCES

In tactical doctrine and weapons, the Japanese Army was ill prepared to defend against a mobile, combined arms force in the open country of central Burma. The topography and terrain of northern Burma, where the dense jungle mitigated, to a degree, the disparity in weapons, allowed the Japanese to employ their infantry tactics to advantage. In the battle for Meiktila, mobility and firepower would dominate the fighting. The Japanese units hurriedly thrust into the battle would find the combination of the two devastating.

The Japanese Army in World War II was an infantry army. Japan's industrial base did not have the capacity to build and support a mechanized army equipped with heavy weapons and tanks, nor did it have the capacity to produce the Army's standard weapons, beyond small arms, in anywhere near adequate quantities, much less produce improved versions. The Army had to base its tactical doctrine on its main strength – the infantry. The basis of Japanese infantry doctrine was an aggressive offense. Japanese doctrine put heavy emphasis on rapid movement and maneuver, to quickly engage an enemy force at close quarters, with envelopment the favored method of attack. Officers and soldiers were imbued with a belief in the power of the offensive spirit, that a resolute force with superior spiritual power could overcome the material advantages of the enemy. The Japanese soldier exhibited a tenacity that other armies found difficult to

Despite a disparity in weapons and equipment, the Japanese infantry soldier was a disciplined, tenacious fighter trained in the spirit of offense and used to hardship. These same troops who had marched with such confidence through central Burma in 1942 now had to cope with the ignominy of retreat. (Author's collection)

The Model 92 70mm howitzer was the standard infantry support weapon at the battalion level. Seen here in action in the Philippines in 1942, the Model 92 was an effective weapon, but its proximity to the front lines made it vulnerable to Allied tanks in the more open Burmese central plain. (Author's collection)

comprehend and often impossible to equal. This faith in the superiority of the offensive led the Japanese Army to inculcate in its officers the belief that a simple plan, rapidly and vigorously executed, was preferable to more deliberate action. Japanese officers were taught to maintain the initiative in battle or, having lost it, to bend every effort to regaining the initiative and return to the offensive. The result of this tactical doctrine in the battles around Meiktila was often a lack of coordination between units in attack, and attacks by units in insufficient strength.

The Japanese forces defending Meiktila, as well as the divisions sent to retake the town, lacked firepower. While reasonably well supplied with small arms and machine guns, they did not have enough artillery and tanks, and those available were less powerful than their British equivalents. Worse still, the Japanese Army was exceptionally weak in anti-tank weapons. The standard infantry division was equipped with 18 Type 92 70mm guns at the battalion level, 12 Type 41 75mm regimental guns in regimental artillery companies, and 36 Type 94 75mm mountain guns or Type 38 or Type 90 75mm field guns in an attached artillery regiment.

Japanese tanks were no match for the Sherman. The Model 95 *Ha-Go*, seen here in Java early in the war, was the Japanese Army's standard light tank. Armed with only a 37mm gun, at Meiktila the *14th Tank Regiment's* Model 95 tanks often fought from dug-in positions. (Author's collection)

These were augmented by medium artillery regiments with combinations of Type 91 105mm howitzers, Type 92 105mm guns, Type 89 150mm guns, or Type 96 150mm howitzers. All were well-built, serviceable weapons, but there were simply too few. The divisions that had fought in the Imphal battles had suffered heavy losses in artillery, which had not been made good. The two divisions ordered to retake Meiktila went into battle with half the standard complement of artillery pieces.

The *14th Tank Regiment*, the only Japanese tank regiment in Burma, went into the Meiktila battles with about one-third of its assigned strength. Despite obtaining reinforcements from Rangoon, the Regiment had only 13 Type 95 *Ha-Go* light tanks and 16 Type 97 *Chi-Ha* medium tanks. With weaker armor and less powerful guns, neither could take on an M4 Sherman with much hope of success, so the Japanese tank crews avoided tank-versus-tank actions whenever possible. After the war the commanding officer of the regiment recalled his shock at seeing the width of a Sherman tank's tracks for the first time, when he came across the imprint a Sherman had left in the ground north of Meiktila. Japanese tank doctrine favored the use of tanks as close support for infantry, to provide covering fire in infantry attacks, but the *14th Tank Regiment* could only employ small numbers of tanks in this role, limiting their effectiveness.

The Japanese Army lacked an effective anti-tank gun. The Type 97 37mm anti-tank gun was completely ineffective against the Sherman, while the newer Type 1 47mm anti-tank gun could only penetrate the Sherman's armor at ranges under 500 yards (455m). To counter tank attacks, the Japanese used a layered defense employing special infantry tank-fighting teams, anti-tank guns, and regimental and divisional artillery. Excellent camouflage and the use of obstacles to restrict tank movement and visibility were critical. The tank-fighting teams were drawn from a company's best infantry soldiers and were taught to engage enemy tanks at close quarters. As the Japanese Army had no equivalent to the bazooka or Panzerfaust, the only weapons available to the teams were mines, incendiary grenades, or other explosives. Under cover of smoke the tank fighting teams would attempt to close with the tanks to disable their tracks, set engines on fire, or climb on the tank to disable the crew inside. All too often this proved to

The Japanese Army lacked an anti-tank gun that could deal with the more powerful Allied tanks of the late-war period. The Model 1 47mm anti-tank gun could only penetrate a Sherman tank's amour at dangerously close range. (PRO WO208/1292)

An abandoned Ki.43 *Hayabusa* fighter of the *64th Sentai* at Mingaladon airfield outside Rangoon. The *64th Sentai* spent almost the entire war on the Burma front, but by 1945 its Ki.43 fighter could do little against the more powerful Spitfires and Thunderbolts. (IWM CI 1352)

be a suicidal mission. As the enemy tanks approached Japanese defensive positions, they would be taken under fire by concealed anti-tank guns, and then 70mm or 75mm mountain guns or field artillery, quickly moved to forward positions. At Meiktila Japanese artillery gunners did employ special hollow-charge shells called *Ta-Dan* to good effect against the Shermans, but the short ranges involved often gave the gun's position away, leading to its destruction by other accompanying tanks.

Of the two Japanese divisions that did most of the fighting around Meiktila, the *18th Division* was a veteran unit with a proud reputation. Having fought in China for four years, the *18th Division* participated in the invasion of Malaya and the capture of Singapore before transferring to Burma where the Division captured Mandalay. The Division then spent two years fighting in northern Burma. When ordered to recapture Meiktila, the Division was at a little more than half strength, with approximately 9,000 men under command, including two under-strength regiments from other divisions. The *49th Division*, the second of the two divisions that played a central role in the battle, was a newer unit that had only arrived in Burma in July of 1944, where it came under the direct command of *Burma Area Army*. The division did not fight as a unit; its regiments were used as reserves to reinforce other divisions. Two of the Division's regiments fought at Meiktila, and both were close to their established strength as the battle began.

The Japanese Army Air Force (JAAF) made a negligible contribution to the battle. A relentless counter-air campaign by the RAF and the USAAF and the demands of other theaters had sharply reduced the number of Japanese aircraft in Burma. By February 1945, the JAAF's *5th Hikoshidan*, responsible for air operations in Burma, Thailand, and French Indochina, had only one air brigade in Burma, the *4th Hikodan*, which controlled the *64th Sentai* with some 20 Type 1 fighters (Allied codename "Oscar"), the *8th Sentai* with 10 Type 98 light bombers ("Lily"), and the *81st Sentai* with 8 Type 100 reconnaissance aircraft ("Dinah"). A small operational training unit, the *7th Rensei Hikotai* had 10 Type 3 fighters ("Tony") for the defense of Rangoon. Constant bombing and strafing of airfields in central Burma had forced the *4th Hikodan* to pull its aircraft back to airfields around Rangoon, further limiting their effectiveness. The limited aircraft available were not used with much imagination. *Burma Area Army* insisted that the *64th Sentai's* fighters undertake ground attack missions, for which the Type 1 fighter was not well-suited, to help boost the infantry's morale. **27**

The fighters might have had a far greater impact had they concentrated on attacking the vulnerable Allied transports.

Notwithstanding the shortages and disparity in guns, tanks, and aircraft, the Japanese soldiers at Meiktila fought with a ferocious tenacity. Few surrendered, and most fought to the last man and the last round.

BRITISH FORCES

The 14th Army that re-entered Burma at the end of 1944 was completely different in strength and spirit from the shattered force that had retreated back to India in 1942. The resurrection of 14th Army was one of the greatest transformations in military history. In the aftermath of the 1942 retreat and the disastrous battles in the Arakan in early 1943, morale of the British and Indian troops was near rock bottom. Poor tactics, a lack of material, rampant disease, and a belief that the Japanese soldier was impossible to defeat in jungle warfare all contributed to a general feeling of hopelessness. When Lieutenant-General Slim took over command of what would soon be re-named 14th Army in October 1943, he realized that to make his army effective each of these problems would have to be addressed, especially the morale of his troops.

Fortunately for Slim, that effort was already underway. General Sir Claude Auchinleck, who had become Commander-in-Chief in India in June of 1943, had instituted a thorough revision in infantry training to give Indian and British troops far tougher and more realistic training in jungle warfare. The problem of inadequate lines of communication from the supply centers in India to the front lines in Assam and the Arakan was slowly, but steadily overcome. As more transport aircraft became available in the theater, air supply took on an ever-increasing share of the logistics burden. In the fall of 1943 British and Indian infantry divisions were re-organized to better equip them for jungle warfare, which also reduced the strain on the supply system. The total number of vehicles was reduced to a minimum, while more animal transport was added. One artillery regiment in each division was converted to a mountain regiment with mortars and mountain guns, while at the battalion level anti-aircraft and anti-tank gun units were eliminated. Tactics were also revised, with much greater emphasis on aggressive patrolling in the jungle rather than passive defense. To counter the favored Japanese tactic of envelopment, British and Indian units were instructed to hold fast in their positions and use the superior firepower they could call on, and better supply through air transport, to wear down the Japanese. As all these changes were being put into place, Slim worked hard to rebuild his army's morale. He gave the 14th Army a mission – the destruction of the Japanese Army in Burma – then set

The Indian Army that marched back into Burma at the end of 1944 had come a long way from the defeated force that had marched out two years earlier. Better trained and better armed, the Army was confident it could defeat the Japanese. Here mountain gunners of the 24th Indian Mountain Artillery regiment carry a 3.7in. howitzer up to the front. (IWM IND 4148)

about convincing his troops that they could do it. The battles in the defense of the Arakan, Kohima, and Imphal in 1944 demonstrated beyond doubt that the efforts of Auchinleck, Slim, and many others had been successful.

The Indian Army provided the bulk of 14th Army's battalions. Of the five divisions that crossed the Chindwin to advance on Mandalay and Meiktila, only one, the 2nd Division, was wholly British. The four other divisions were all Indian Infantry Divisions, as was the 5th Indian Infantry Division in reserve. Nearly all the Indian Army's regiments were represented in 14th Army. There were Gurkha, Baluch, Rajput, Dogra, Jat, and Sikh battalions, and battalions from Bengal, Hyderabad, Punjab, and Madras. In addition to its Indian battalions, each one of an Indian division's three brigades had one British battalion. There were British and Indian artillery regiments, sappers, and tank regiments. Slim had molded this disparate group with its multiplicity of languages, religions, and diets into a cohesive, coordinated force. The divisions, brigades, and battalions were well led, their soldiers experienced and confident. Slim now had the right instrument to achieve his ultimate goal, and the right terrain where he could bring 14th Army's advantages in artillery, tanks, and air support to bear to hammer the Japanese.

The divisions fighting in the Irrawaddy battles typically had two field artillery regiments and one Indian mountain artillery regiment for artillery support. Standard equipment for the field artillery regiments in Burma was the excellent 25-pdr field gun, which fired a heavier shell at longer ranges than the Japanese 75mm guns. Each regiment had three batteries with six guns each. The Indian mountain artillery regiments were equipped with 12 to 16 3.7in. howitzers or 3in. mortars. A division would have an anti-tank regiment on strength as well, with 36 6-pdr anti-tank guns. In the absence of Japanese tanks the anti-tank regiments added mortar companies with 36 3in. mortars. The infantry battalions

In the hands of Major-General Cowan's two aggressive Indian tank regiments, the Sherman tank proved to be the decisive weapon in the battle for Meiktila, working closely with the infantry. (IWM SE 3094 FAR EAST 14V)

normally had a mortar platoon attached with six additional 3in. mortars. A British or Indian infantry division could throw out a greater weight of fire than its Japanese counterpart. The capability was made all the more effective through better radio communication and fire coordination. The Japanese greatly admired the British 3in. mortar, which proved excellent for close-in fighting, and more effective than the Japanese battalion and regimental guns.

The decisive weapon in the Meiktila battles proved to be the tank. In post-war interrogations, Japanese officers said that in the fighting around Meiktila tanks caused by far the greatest number of casualties in men and guns. The Japanese were never able to develop effective countermeasures against British tanks. Slim had two Indian tank brigades in 14th Army, the veteran 254th Indian Tank Brigade, equipped with Lee and Grant tanks, and the 255th Indian Tank Brigade, which had not seen combat but was equipped with the more capable Sherman tank. He assigned the 254th Tank Brigade to XXXIII Corps, and gave the more powerful Shermans of 255th Tank Brigade to IV Corps for the thrust to Meiktila. This would be a new type of fighting for 14th Army. Tanks had been used, in small numbers, to good effect in the jungle. The terrain around Meiktila was good tank country; open, dry plains and rolling hills, with mostly scrub brush and trees providing limited concealment. Here troops of tanks with mechanized infantry in support could travel with relative freedom of movement. What the fighting did require was close cooperation between tanks and infantry. With their restricted visibility, the tanks had to rely on the infantry to help spot Japanese positions and to defend against the Japanese anti-tank teams. There had not been time for extensive training in tank/infantry tactics, which led to some errors in deployment and execution, but both groups learned quickly. Each tank had a telephone behind the engine for communication between the accompanying infantry and the tank crew, but under fire this was not always safe to use. Nor was it safe, in these circumstances, for the tank commander to climb out of his turret to talk with the infantry. After a few

Air supply made it possible for General Slim to push 14th Army deep into Burma. The C-47s of the 1st and 2nd Air Commando Groups flew many missions in support of IV Corps. Here a C-47 of the 319th Transport Squadron, 1st Air Commando Group, gets refueled. (National Archives 342-FH-3A-35875-A61277AC)

A P-47D of the 1st Air Commando Group next to a P-51D of the newly arrived 2nd Air Commando Group at Cox's Bazar near Chittagong. The Air Commando fighter squadrons flew constantly in support of IV Corps during the battle for Meiktila. (Author's collection)

encounters with the Japanese, the tank unit commanders worked out some basic signals with their infantry counterparts to help the two groups communicate in the noise and limited visibility of close-quarters fighting. With experience, the tank crews learned to recognize the direction of Japanese fire and identify likely Japanese positions. The tank crews became expert at bunker busting and breaking up Japanese attacks. Japanese units caught in the open suffered heavily.

In the air, the RAF and the USAAF had established a level of air superiority amounting to air supremacy. Air superiority allowed 14th Army to be heavily dependent on air supply with little fear that this supply line would be disrupted. Not having to provide escort to the transport planes meant that the fighters could concentrate on close air support and interdiction. To support 14th Army in the coming battle, the RAF had No. 221 Group with eight squadrons of Hurricanes (two for tactical reconnaissance), three Thunderbolt squadrons, three Beaufighter and Mosquito squadrons for long-range interdiction, and four Spitfire squadrons for air defense over the battlefield. 14th Army could also call on the fighter squadrons of No. 224 Group in the Arakan, and the USAAF's 12th Bombardment Group with four squadrons of B-25 Mitchell medium bombers.

To provide even more support during its critical thrust to Meiktila and the expected defense of the town, IV Corps arranged with the Combat Cargo Task Force to have the fighter squadrons of the CCTF's 1st and 2nd Air Commando Groups assigned directly to IV Corps. This gave IV Corps the 1st Air Commando Group's two P-47 Thunderbolt squadrons and the two P-51D Mustang squadrons of the recently arrived 2nd Air Commando Group, a total of approximately 100 fighters. The 1st Air Commando Group fighters would provide 'cab rank' patrols throughout the day over the mechanized columns as they pushed toward Meiktila. In a new tactic, the fighters would work with Visual Control Points (VCPs), an RAF officer riding in a jeep with the advancing columns who was in radio contact with the fighters. The 2nd Air Commando Group's Mustangs flew beyond Meiktila to strike at Japanese assembly points and supplies.

ORDERS OF BATTLE

JAPANESE FORCES – BURMA THEATER, JANUARY 1945

Burma Area Army	LtGen H. Kimura
15th Army	***LtGen S. Katamura***
15th Division	LtGen R. Shibata
31st Division	LtGen T. Kawada
33rd Division	LtGen N. Tanaka
213th Infantry Regiment	
214th Infantry Regiment	
215th Infantry Regiment	
53rd Division	LtGen K. Takeda
119th Infantry Regiment	
128th Infantry Regiment	
151st Infantry Regiment	
14th Tank Regiment	
28th Army	***LtGen S. Sakurai***
54th Division	LtGen S. Miyazaki
55th Division	LtGen T. Sakuma
72nd Independent Mixed Brigade	MajGen T. Yamamoto
33rd Army	***LtGen M. Honda***
18th Division	LtGen E. Naka
55th Infantry Regiment	
56th Infantry Regiment	
114th Infantry Regiment	
56th Division	LtGen Y. Matsuyama
Reserves	
49th Division	LtGen S. Takehara
106th Infantry Regiment	
153rd Infantry Regiment	
168th Infantry Regiment	
24th Independent Mixed Brigade	MajGen Y. Hayashi
2nd Division	
16th Regiment	

BRITISH & COMMONWEALTH FORCES – BURMA THEATER

14th Army	LtGen Sir William Slim
IV Corps	***LtGen Frank Messervy***
7th Indian Infantry Division	MajGen G.C. Evans
17th Indian Infantry Division	MajGen D.T. Cowan
48th Indian Infantry Brigade	
63rd Indian Infantry Brigade	
99th Indian Infantry Brigade	
255th Indian Tank Brigade	Brig C.E. Pert
116th Regiment, Royal Armoured Corps	
5th (Probyn's) Horse	
9th (Royal Deccan) Horse	
16th Light Cavalry	
28th East African Brigade	Brig W.A. Dimoline
Lushai Brigade	Brig P.C. Marindin
XXXIII Corps	***LtGen Sir Montague Stopford***
2nd Division	MajGen C.G.C. Nicholson
19th Indian Infantry Division	MajGen T.W. Rees
20th Indian Infantry Division	MajGen D.D. Gracey
254th Indian Tank Brigade	Brig R.L. Scoones
268th Indian Infantry Brigade	Brig G.M. Dyer
Reserves	
5th Indian Infantry Division	MajGen E.C.R. Mansergh

THE MEIKTILA CAMPAIGN

THE ADVANCE TO THE IRRAWADDY

When Slim met with Messervy and Stopford, his two corps commanders, on 18 December to explain his new plan, he impressed on them the need to press forward as rapidly as possible. Timing was critical to the success of "Extended Capital". Slim's ultimate goal, assuming he could defeat Kimura's armies around Mandalay and Meiktila, was to exploit this success and advance south to Rangoon. To sustain 14th Army's campaign beyond the central plains, Slim needed to capture a port in southern Burma before the onset of the monsoon in early May. The monsoon season dictated the timing of the battles. Slim's original target dates were for IV Corps and XXXIII Corps to close up to the Irrawaddy River by the end of January, and to capture Mandalay and Meiktila by the end of February. This was an aggressive timetable given the administrative and logistical hurdles to be overcome, but 14th Army came close to meeting these dates. Slim told Messervy and Stopford to get started, and set 26 December as the date for the transfer of divisions between the two corps.

"Extended Capital" had a lesser impact on XXXIII Corps as its newly assigned units were more or less in place to begin their advance. By the third week of December, 19th Division was the farthest east, having captured Pinlebu, 2nd Division had crossed the Chindwin at Kalewa and was moving east, while 20th Division was also across and advancing on 2nd Division's right flank. 268th Brigade had also moved across the

The road from Imphal to Tamu, part of the minimal road system from Assam into northern Burma that made 14th Army so dependent on air transport. (IWM IND 3711)

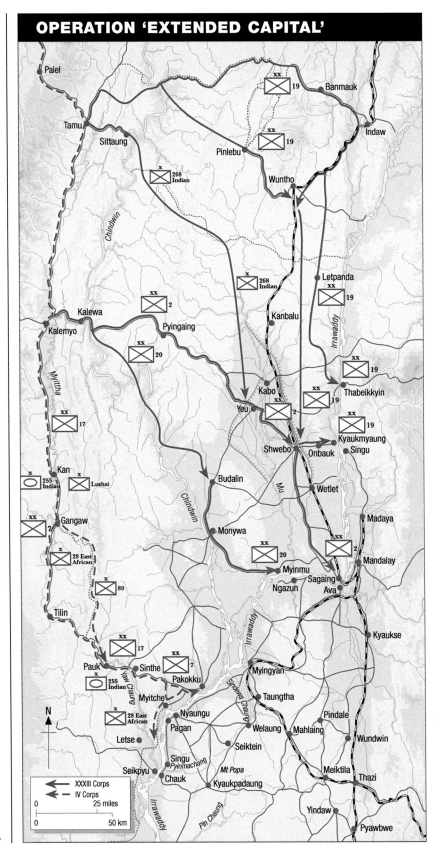

A Bailey bridge across the Chindwin River. At one point this was the longest Bailey bridge in the world. All the sections had to be carried across the mountains to the Chindwin. (IWM SE 2827)

Chindwin, while 254th Tank Brigade was concentrating its units in preparation for crossing to the east bank. On 20 December, Stopford met with his division commanders and assigned them their new tasks. XXXIII Corps' objective was to advance on a broad front to the Irrawaddy, mimicking 14th Army's original plan. Stopford ordered 19th Division to be XXXIII Corps' left flank, advancing down the west bank of the Irrawaddy to attack Shwebo from the east. 2nd Division would occupy the center of the advance, and approach Shwebo from the west. Together the two divisions would capture the town and its vital airfields, which would be critical to the advance as the existing roads were incapable of sustaining the entire Corps. Once Shwebo had been captured, 19th Division would turn east and seize bridgeheads across the Irrawaddy north of Mandalay, while 2nd Division moved further south to the Irrawaddy bend around Sagaing. On the right flank, 20th Division would move down the Chindwin to capture Monywa, and then advance to the Irrawaddy to make a crossing and advance on Mandalay from the southwest. Slim hoped that 19th Division's association with IV Corps would lead the Japanese to believe that the entire 14th Army was advancing on Mandalay, and that multiple crossings to the north and south of the city would draw Kimura's attention away from IV Corps' real advance. To aid in the deception, Slim had a dummy IV Corps headquarters remain in place after Messervy had moved the axis of his advance to the west, and funneled all radio communications between XXXIII Corps and 19th Division through this dummy HQ.

IV Corps had the far more daunting task. The route from Tamu, where the advance would begin, to Pakokku on the Irrawaddy River, where IV Corps would seize a crossing, was roughly 320 miles (515km). From Tamu to Kalemyo the road was reasonable, though under a heavy layer of dust, but beyond Kalemyo the route turned into a narrow single-lane road that after some 90 miles (145km) turned into a dirt track. Neither road nor track was capable of supporting heavy trucks or tank transporters. The track went over steep hills with hairpin turns, and across streams with inadequate bridges or no bridges at all. In the rain the track quickly turned to deep mud, and in the dry season to dust a foot deep. To compound the

Once across the Chindwin, pagodas became a familiar sight as the 14th Army entered the central plain. (IWM IND 4283)

35

problem, the units assigned to IV Corps were strung out from the Myittha Valley back to India. The Lushai Brigade, near Gangaw, was in closest contact with the enemy. 7th Division, which would lead the advance, was spread out from Tamu back to Kohima, the 28th East African Brigade, 16th Cavalry, and 255th Tank Brigade were at Imphal, and 17th Division was resting at Ranchi, west of Calcutta. All these units and their equipment would have to be brought forward in stages to concentration points near Pakokku, over a road that had yet to be built. To reduce traffic over the already over-burdened route, IV Corps would be entirely dependent on air supply during its advance, which meant that the engineers would need to build rough airstrips along the route as well as improving the track. Slim insisted that the advance be conducted under strict radio silence, putting additional burdens on staff officers trying to coordinate the movement of an entire corps spread out over 300 miles (483km).

Havildar Raldon, a Chin volunteer with the Lushai Brigade that led the advance down the Myittha Valley and captured Gangaw. (IWM IND 4265)

Messervy's basic plan was to have the Lushai Brigade, composed of Lushai and Chin levies with regular Indian Army battalions attached, to advance and capture Gangaw where the Japanese *33rd Division* had left a small, but well-entrenched rear guard. Beyond Gangaw the 28th East African Brigade would lead the advance to make the Japanese think this unit was part of the 11th East African Division, which had been advancing down the Kawbaw Valley before being withdrawn at the end of December, and which the Japanese knew to be attached to XXXIII Corps. 7th Division would follow 28th East African Brigade in stages, far enough behind so as not to encounter the Japanese rearguards. The Division would concentrate at Kan until Gangaw was taken, then move down the valley to Tilin, and from Tilin to Pauk. When the track down the valley had been sufficiently improved, 255th Tank Brigade would begin its advance to a concentration area near the Irrawaddy River followed by 17th Division, which would be brought up right before the crossing. Messervy told his engineers that the track had to be ready to support tanks by 31 January 1945. Once out of the Myittha Valley, 7th Division would seize Pakokku, clear the west bank of the Irrawaddy, and seize a bridgehead across the river. The assault force, 17th Division and 255th Tank Brigade, would then cross and race for Meiktila.

Messervy wasted no time. The day after his return from his conference with Slim, he ordered all of IV Corps' engineers to start improving the road and track south of Kalemyo at once. The lightly armed Lushai Brigade had no artillery, which would be needed for the fight at Gangaw. Messervy's first priority was to improve the track sufficiently to send down a field artillery regiment with 25-pdrs to join the Lushai Brigade near Gangaw. It took 7th Division's engineers two weeks of hard work to get the track ready, but by the end of the month field artillery Quads were on their way to Gangaw. The troops started moving before the 26 December handover date as well, the 28th East African Brigade leaving Imphal on 22 December, followed by 7th Division. Trucks carried the battalions to the Chindwin, and after crossing the river on ferries the troops set out on foot down the Myittha Valley.

An RAF Dakota drops supplies in the Myittha Valley. During its advance 7th Indian Division had to rely on air supply drops as the track down the valley could not support the number of vehicles needed to bring supplies forward by road. (IWM HU 1162)

Unexpectedly heavy rains during the first week of January brought all transport along the route to a complete halt and delayed the Lushai Brigade's attack on Gangaw. This was rescheduled for 10 January and, to ensure that the town was captured without delay, Messervy laid on an "Earthquake" bombardment mission. He and Slim flew in to watch the show. At 14.00hrs the USAAF 12th Bombardment Group sent in four squadrons of B-25 Mitchell bombers to bomb selected targets in and around the town. When the dust had cleared, 24 Hurricanes and 12 Thunderbolts went in by sections to bomb and strafe Japanese positions, followed by dummy runs as the Lushai Brigade's troops advanced into the town under covering artillery fire. A further 10 Hurricanes flew overhead on "cab-rank" patrol. After a brief fight the Japanese troops pulled back, and the town was completely cleared the next day. With the capture of Gangaw the Lushai Brigade switched back to scouting 7th Division's flanks, while 28th East African Brigade took over the advance. On 12 December, the East Africans started south out of Gangaw, while the rest of 7th Division converged on the Division concentration area at Kan.

To the east, XXXIII Corps' divisions had made rapid progress despite some skillful rearguard actions on the part of the Japanese. On the left flank, 19th Division advanced in three columns and reached Kanlebu, the gateway to the Shwebo plain, on 2 January to find that the Japanese had abandoned the town. This enabled the Division to push on rapidly for Shwebo from the north and east. The British 2nd Division had captured Yeu on 3 January after a tough fight then, under air cover, crossed the Mu River and closed in on Shwebo from the northwest. The two divisions made contact and initiated a joint attack on 8 January against three battalions of the *31st Division*. The town was cleared on 10 January, with the Japanese forces retreating south to Sagaing. That same day 20th Division captured Budalin and then pushed on to Monywa, a key administrative center and port on the Chindwin River that the Japanese were determined to defend. The Japanese had underestimated the force approaching the town, and with priority given to getting the bulk of *Burma Area Army's* units back across the Irrawaddy, they left the defense of Monywa to two battalions from the *33rd Division* and one from the *31st Division*. These battalions had, however, dug strong positions on the northern and eastern approaches to the town. Following the success of the Gangaw "Earthquake", XXXIII Corps arranged for a similar intensive attack on the Japanese positions at Monywa. On 20 January, following an

The 2nd British Division captured Shwebo on 8 January 1945. A Bren gun carrier moves through the town following its capture. (IWM SE 1379)

IV AND XXXIII CORPS CROSSINGS OF THE IRRAWADDY RIVER

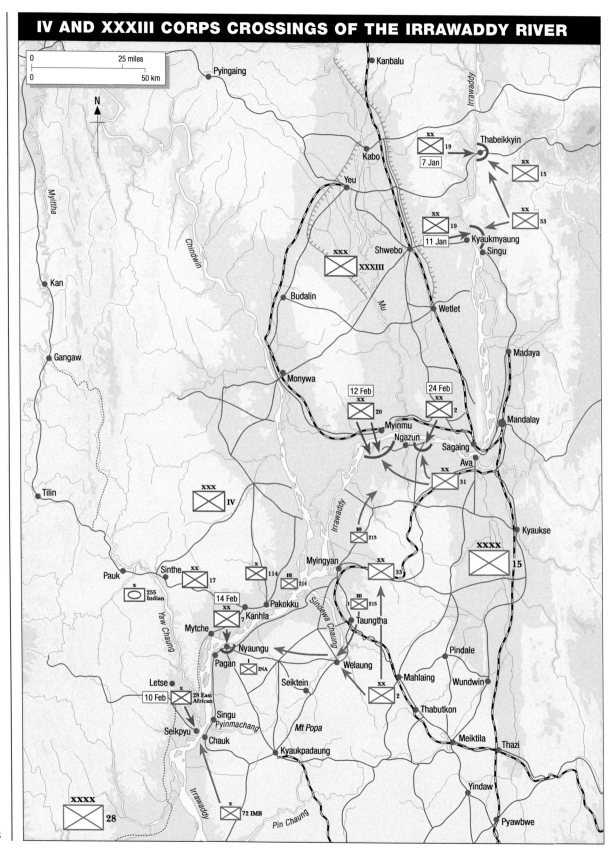

artillery barrage, No. 221 Group sent in 13 Mosquitos to bomb the Japanese positions with 500lb bombs, followed by seven rocket-firing Hurricanes, and then six Thunderbolts with more bombs. While these attacks did not carry enough weight to destroy the Japanese bunkers, they did weaken the defenders sufficiently to enable 20th Division's attack to penetrate the town, which was occupied on the 22nd.

While helping to capture Shwebo, 19th Division had sent one brigade to occupy the west bank of the Irrawaddy at Thabeikkyin and Kyauk-myaung, north of Mandalay. On 9 January the brigade sent patrols across the river and quickly established bridgeheads. Over the next week 19th Division steadily expanded the forces within the two bridgeheads and by 19 January had one full brigade in the bridgehead opposite Kyaukmyaung. General Katamura, commander of *15th Army*, viewed this development with alarm. By early January he had successfully withdrawn most of his depleted forces back across the Irrawaddy and set them up in

their allocated defensive positions north and south of Mandalay. The intelligence he had on 14th Army's forces arrayed against him was inadequate. In line with Japanese Army doctrine and not realizing the full extent of the force bearing down on *15th Army*, *Burma Area Army* was planning a counter-offensive back across the Irrawaddy when 19th Division established its bridgeheads. With *Burma Area Army's* concurrence, Katamura decided to destroy these bridgeheads before they could become entrenched. He ordered the *15th Division* to send a force to contain the bridgehead at Thabeikkyin, while the remainder of the division and additional forces from the *53rd Division* devoted the greater part of their effort to eliminating the bridgehead at Kyaukmyaung. In a series of night attacks during the last week of January the Japanese hurled themselves at 19th Division's positions around Kyaukmyaung where the British and Indian troops were by now well-dug in with strong artillery and machine gun support. Both *15th* and *53rd Divisions* were under strength, but rather than concentrating their limited forces for greater power, the attacks were mounted by one or two platoons, with reinforcements being fed into the assault as they arrived. The heaviest attack took place on the night of 30/31 January, when the bridgehead was subject to exceptionally heavy shelling by 70mm, 105mm, and 150mm guns, the Japanese having brought up more than 30 artillery pieces. Repeated attacks were beaten back throughout the night. In a week of fighting *15th Division* lost one-third of its strength.

As Slim had intended, XXXIII Corps' advance across a broad front distracted the Japanese from IV Corps' march down the Myittha Valley. *Burma Area Army* did receive vague reports of movement on 14th Army's far right flank, and one aerial report of a long column of vehicles, but coming in the midst of reports of attacks all along the front these reports were never followed up. In the meantime, Messervy had halted the advance at Gangaw to allow IV Corps' forward units to be re-supplied and to give 7th Division's three brigades time to move forward. He ordered the advance to begin again on 19 January, and on that date 28th East African Brigade set out from Gangaw followed by 114th Brigade, which marched far enough behind the East Africans to avoid running into any Japanese rearguards. So as not to overburden the track, Major-General G.C. Evans, 7th Division commander, sent the 89th Brigade on a long left hook down to Pauk, paralleling the advance. He designated his third brigade, the 33rd, to make the initial crossing of the Irrawaddy, and ordered the brigade to stay in Gangaw to practice with the assault boats that were to be used in the crossing. The 28th East African Brigade encountered little resistance, but in places the Japanese had cut hundreds of trees down across the track to slow the advance. These had to be removed with the help of local elephants and the Quad gun trucks from the artillery. The Brigade reached Tilin on 23 January, while the 89th Brigade occupied Pauk on the 28th.

While 7th Division worked its way down toward the Irrawaddy, Messervy and his IV Corps staff worked out the final plans for the attack on Meiktila with his two division commanders, Evans and Cowan. On 17 January, Slim had given Messervy formal orders to seize a bridgehead across the Irrawaddy, get the assault force across, and seize Meiktila. Slim called for "speed, surprise, and punch". The first step was to cross the Irrawaddy. Messervy chose the crossing point on the Irrawaddy with great care. He had to balance the need for surprise and speed with the practical difficulties the terrain along the Irrawaddy's banks imposed on him. He had only a limited number of assault boats and rafts available to him for the crossing, which put a premium on finding a crossing point where the river was narrowest. From Pakokku to Chauk the Irrawaddy varied from three-quarters of a mile to two miles (1.2–3.2km) in width. Ever changing sandbanks, some below the water line, created multiple channels in the river and limited the number of direct crossing points. Pakokku was the closest point to Meiktila, but Messervy and Evans felt it would be too obvious a crossing point. After studying aerial reconnaissance photos, Evans recommended crossing opposite Nyaungu, a small village a few miles east of Pagan, where the river was only three-quarters of a mile wide. This site was one of the

7th Division had to make its own road as it advanced down the Valley. Teams of elephants helped clear the track so that engineers could lay down a temporary road surface. (IWM HU 1079)

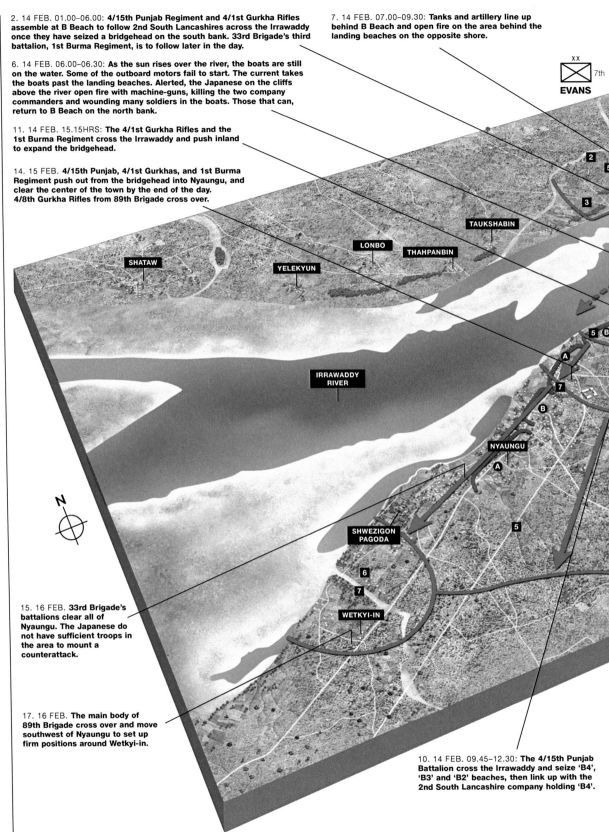

2. 14 FEB. 01.00–06.00: **4/15th Punjab Regiment and 4/1st Gurkha Rifles assemble at B Beach to follow 2nd South Lancashires across the Irrawaddy once they have seized a bridgehead on the south bank. 33rd Brigade's third battalion, 1st Burma Regiment, is to follow later in the day.**

6. 14 FEB. 06.00–06.30: **As the sun rises over the river, the boats are still on the water. Some of the outboard motors fail to start. The current takes the boats past the landing beaches. Alerted, the Japanese on the cliffs above the river open fire with machine-guns, killing the two company commanders and wounding many soldiers in the boats. Those that can, return to B Beach on the north bank.**

11. 14 FEB. 15.15HRS: **The 4/1st Gurkha Rifles and the 1st Burma Regiment cross the Irrawaddy and push inland to expand the bridgehead.**

14. 15 FEB. **4/15th Punjab, 4/1st Gurkhas, and 1st Burma Regiment push out from the bridgehead into Nyaungu, and clear the center of the town by the end of the day. 4/8th Gurkha Rifles from 89th Brigade cross over.**

7. 14 FEB. 07.00–09.30: **Tanks and artillery line up behind B Beach and open fire on the area behind the landing beaches on the opposite shore.**

7th

EVANS

2

3

TAUKSHABIN

LONBO

THAHPANBIN

SHATAW

YELEKYUN

5 **B**

A

7

B

IRRAWADDY RIVER

NYAUNGU

A

5

N

SHWEZIGON PAGODA

6

7

15. 16 FEB. **33rd Brigade's battalions clear all of Nyaungu. The Japanese do not have sufficient troops in the area to mount a counterattack.**

WETKYI-IN

17. 16 FEB. **The main body of 89th Brigade cross over and move southwest of Nyaungu to set up firm positions around Wetkyi-in.**

10. 14 FEB. 09.45–12.30: **The 4/15th Punjab Battalion cross the Irrawaddy and seize 'B4', 'B3' and 'B2' beaches, then link up with the 2nd South Lancashire company holding 'B4'.**

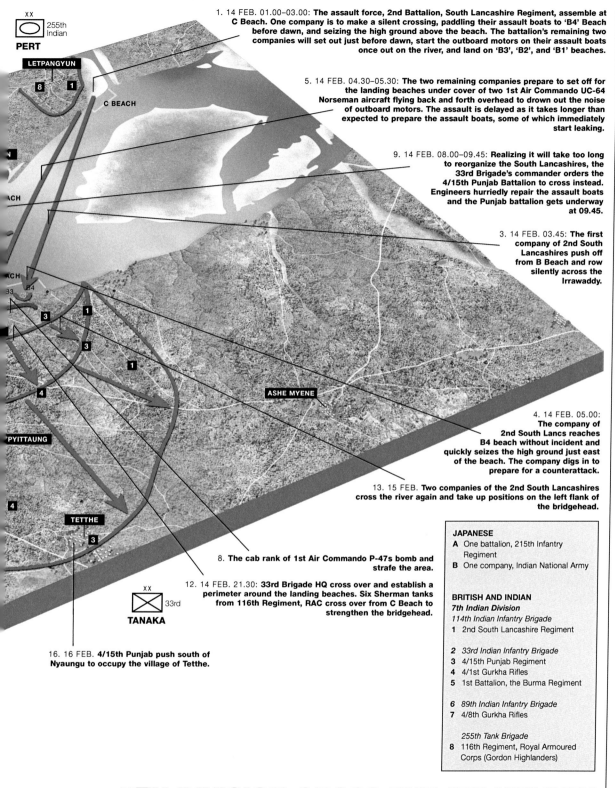

XX
255th Indian
PERT

LETPANGYUN

8 1

C BEACH

N

ACH

ACH

33 B4

3

1

3

3

1

4

ASHE MYENE

PYITTAUNG

4

TETTHE

3

1. 14 FEB. 01.00–03.00: The assault force, 2nd Battalion, South Lancashire Regiment, assemble at C Beach. One company is to make a silent crossing, paddling their assault boats to 'B4' Beach before dawn, and seizing the high ground above the beach. The battalion's remaining two companies will set out just before dawn, start the outboard motors on their assault boats once out on the river, and land on 'B3', 'B2', and 'B1' beaches.

5. 14 FEB. 04.30–05.30: The two remaining companies prepare to set off for the landing beaches under cover of two 1st Air Commando UC-64 Norseman aircraft flying back and forth overhead to drown out the noise of outboard motors. The assault is delayed as it takes longer than expected to prepare the assault boats, some of which immediately start leaking.

9. 14 FEB. 08.00–09.45: Realizing it will take too long to reorganize the South Lancashires, the 33rd Brigade's commander orders the 4/15th Punjab Battalion to cross instead. Engineers hurriedly repair the assault boats and the Punjab battalion gets underway at 09.45.

3. 14 FEB. 03.45: The first company of 2nd South Lancashires push off from B Beach and row silently across the Irrawaddy.

4. 14 FEB. 05.00: The company of 2nd South Lancs reaches B4 beach without incident and quickly seizes the high ground just east of the beach. The company digs in to prepare for a counterattack.

13. 15 FEB. Two companies of the 2nd South Lancashires cross the river again and take up positions on the left flank of the bridgehead.

8. The cab rank of 1st Air Commando P-47s bomb and strafe the area.

12. 14 FEB. 21.30: 33rd Brigade HQ cross over and establish a perimeter around the landing beaches. Six Sherman tanks from 116th Regiment, RAC cross over from C Beach to strengthen the bridgehead.

XX
33rd
TANAKA

16. 16 FEB. 4/15th Punjab push south of Nyaungu to occupy the village of Tetthe.

JAPANESE
A One battalion, 215th Infantry Regiment
B One company, Indian National Army

BRITISH AND INDIAN
7th Indian Division
114th Indian Infantry Brigade
1 2nd South Lancashire Regiment

2 *33rd Indian Infantry Brigade*
3 4/15th Punjab Regiment
4 4/1st Gurkha Rifles
5 1st Battalion, the Burma Regiment

6 *89th Indian Infantry Brigade*
7 4/8th Gurkha Rifles

255th Tank Brigade
8 116th Regiment, Royal Armoured Corps (Gordon Highlanders)

7TH DIVISION CROSS THE IRRAWADDY
14–16 February 1945, viewed from the southwest, showing 7th Division's crossing points, the landing beaches a mile east of Nyaungu, and the bridgehead area up to 16 February 1945.

narrowest crossing points along the river and one of the few where a direct crossing would be possible. Before the war it had been a ferry point. This would enable 17th Division to get across the Irrawaddy at a faster pace once the bridgehead had been established. From Nyaungu, roads ran out to the northeast, east, and south, which would speed the advance on Meiktila. A surprise crossing at this point would, however, be difficult. On the west bank of the Irrawaddy opposite Nyaungu the approach to the river crossed several hundred yards of open sandy beach, making any movement or vehicle easily visible from the cliffs that ran along the Irrawaddy's eastern bank.

Evans instead chose a point about two miles farther upstream where the approach to the river offered more concealment. This meant that the initial crossing would have to be done on a diagonal of well over a mile, making it the longest opposed river crossing attempted during World War II. As IV Corps did not have sufficient artillery ammunition available to support an assault in daylight, Evans and his staff devised a plan to have one battalion make a silent crossing before first light to land on four beaches one mile northeast of Nyaungu. Once this battalion had seized the high ground above the beaches, the rest of 33rd Brigade would follow in powered assault boats and launch an attack on Nyaungu to establish a bridgehead. After 33rd Brigade had consolidated the bridgehead, the rest of 7th Division would cross over using the shorter crossing point at Nyaungu, followed by 17th Division. Evans assigned the assault crossing to the 2nd Battalion, South Lancashire Regiment, which had participated in the invasion of Madagascar in 1942.

Nyaungu had the drawback of being an obvious crossing point. Slim had urged his generals to take risks, and to use deception as much as pos-sible. Messervy and Evans worked out a deception plan, named Operation "Cloak", designed to make the Japanese look away from Nyaungu and think that a major crossing was planned farther south. The plan called for the 114th Brigade to push east and capture the town of Pakokku, to give the impression that this was in preparation for a crossing opposite the town. At the same time, the 28th East African Brigade would push down the west bank of the Irrawaddy to attack the town of Seikpyu opposite Chauk on the route to the vital oilfields at Yenangyaung. A third battalion-size force would make a small but noisy crossing below Pagan. The Japanese would thus be faced with three potential crossings. Messervy set a target date of 15 February for 7th Division to seize the bridgehead at Nyaungu. What neither Messervy nor Evans knew at the time was that they had chosen to cross the Irrawaddy just at the boundary between the Japanese *15th Army* and *28th Army*, and neither army had sought to establish firm contact along this boundary line.

Even if he could achieve a surprise crossing, Messervy knew he still needed speed and punch to seize Meiktila. He recommended to Slim that 17th Division be reorganized into a fully motorized division. The mules that had formed a good part of the Division's transport in the jungle would only slow down the advance once across the Irrawaddy. The route to Meiktila covered dry, dusty ground that would be perfect for tanks and trucks. Slim agreed, but even by taking all available motor transport from the 11th East African Division, then on its way back to India, and some from the 5th Division, there were only enough trucks and other vehicles to completely equip two brigades. Messervy and Major-General

Cowan decided that 17th Division's 48th and 63rd Brigades would be motorized, and its third brigade, the 99th, would be made air-transportable. The latter would be flown into an airfield near Meiktila with the bare minimum of jeeps for transport. This would enable 17th Division to get to Meiktila with all speed, yet with sufficient force to capture and defend the town. When the Division reached Imphal in the third week of January, the three brigades gave up their animal transport and immediately started training in their new roles. Before the tanks of 255th Tank Brigade left Imphal, the 48th and 63rd Brigades had some time, but not much, to practice the combined infantry-tank tactics they would use in the attack. Then 17th Division's two brigades also set off down the Myittha Valley. Messervy had ordered Cowan to have his division ready, in the crossing area, by the date of the crossing.

To the east, Stopford had slowed XXXIII Corps' advance to allow his divisions to build up the supplies they would need for the next stage of the campaign, and to allow 254th Tank Brigade to move up to the front where its tank units were parceled out among the Corps' three divisions. Slim's plan was for XXXIII Corps to give the Japanese the impression that 14th Army was launching an envelopment of Mandalay, and to initiate the attack a few days prior to 7th Division's crossing of the Irrawaddy as a distraction from IV Corps' activities to the west. To this end, 19th Division was ordered to consolidate its two bridgeheads and move on Mandalay from the north, while 20th Division crossed the Irrawaddy opposite Myinmu to approach Mandalay from the west and south. The task of 2nd Division was to eliminate a strong Japanese position at Sagaing, clear all Japanese forces from the bend of the Irrawaddy then, when assault boats were available, cross over to join up with 20th Division for the assault on Mandalay. No. 221 Group took this lull to move its shorter range Hurricane and Spitfire squadrons closer to the front to ensure air superiority over the battlefield, using airfields the Japanese had recently abandoned. To supplement the air transport of supplies, 14th Army arranged to have a fleet of rafts and small boats built with local timber so that supplies could be carried down the Chindwin River to the front.

As soon as it could No. 221 Group, RAF, moved its shorter range Hurricane and Spitfire squadrons closer to the front. A Spitfire takes off from a rough airstrip, with a temporary control tower made from palm trees. (IWM CF 251)

By the first week of February 1945, 14th Army had established itself on the west bank of the Irrawaddy in an arc running from Thabeikkyin in the east to Myitche in the west. On 5 February, LtGen Messervy gave his final orders to IV Corps for the crossing of the Irrawaddy and the thrust to Meiktila, which he had named "Operation Multivite". The first phase, "Vitamin A", was the seizure of Pakokku and the concentration of 17th Division at Pauk; "Vitamin B" was the establishment of the bridgehead across the Irrawaddy, "Vitamin C" the concentration of 7th and 17th Divisions on the eastern bank of the Irrawaddy, and "Vitamin D" the lightening advance to Meiktila. The deception forces set out first, 28th East African Brigade heading down the west bank of the Irrawaddy toward Seikpyu, and 114th Brigade to Pakokku, while 89th Brigade finished clearing the area around Myitche, and 33rd Brigade finished preparations for the initial crossing. Work continued at a feverish pace, as the deadline for the crossing was less than ten days away. When the assault craft arrived in the area, many were found to have been damaged in transit, necessitating hurried repairs. 17th Division and 255th Tank Brigade were working their way down to their concentration area around Pauk, the tanks traveling on their own tracks as the worn out tank transporters could not traverse the track past Kan. The shuttling of troops, trucks, and tanks towards Pauk never let up.

The road from Pauk to Pakokku went through a road junction at the small village of Kanhla, where the *214th Regiment* had established a rearguard on the hills overlooking the junction. As 33rd Brigade had to pass through Kanhla on the way to its assembly points for the assault crossing, 114th Brigade's first objective on the way to Pakokku was to clear the Japanese from Kanhla. The Japanese were well dug in, and it was not until 10 February that the village and surrounding hills were cleared. The assault force could now proceed to the Irrawaddy undetected. Slim gave the order for both IV Corps and XXXIII Corps to begin their advance. Anticipating an attack on Mandalay, General Kimura had no inkling that his armies were about to be caught in the trap Slim had so carefully prepared for them.

THE ATTACK ON MEIKTILA

After 10 February, fighting erupted across the entire front. Over the next four days attacks and feints came in rapid succession, as Slim had planned. On 14th Army's left flank, 19th Division pushed out of its bridgehead at Kyaukmyaung to capture Singu. Rees' orders to his division were "On to Mandalay". On the right flank, 28th East African Brigade closed on Seikpyu and launched a series of attacks, capturing the town on 12 February. The *72 Independent Mixed Brigade*, charged with guarding the oilfields at Yenangyaung, reacted strongly to the attack on Seikpyu, immediately sending a battalion and two companies of the *153rd Regiment* across the Irrawaddy to counterattack and clear the town. In several days of heavy fighting the *153rd Regiment* forced 28th East African Brigade to fall back toward Letse, but the Brigade's feint had achieved its purpose in drawing off the Japanese forces around the Nyaungu area. Near 7th Division's crossing point, 114th Brigade held off a series of counter-attacks on Kanhla, then pushed on to Pakokku, where elements of the

Stuart tanks of the 7th Indian Light Cavalry Regiment cross the Irrawaddy with 20th Division, 13 February 1945. (IWM IND 4461)

After a near disaster in the early morning hours of 14 February 1945, 7th Division managed to establish a firm bridgehead at Nyaungu by mid-afternoon. Troops and supplies continued to be ferried across the Irrawaddy throughout the day. (IWM HU 1073)

214th Regiment put up fierce resistance. With the aid of tanks and air strikes, 114th Brigade captured the town. Then, on the night of 12 February, 20th Division began crossing the Irrawaddy a few miles west of Myinmu, with the objective of approaching Mandalay from the west to cut the Mandalay–Meiktila road. By mid-morning on the 13th, the Division had sent across three battalions to establish two bridgeheads on the east bank. These linked up a few days later. From the Japanese perspective it appeared that 14th Army's envelopment of Mandalay had begun, as expected, with a new thrust down the west bank of the Irrawaddy (which was not seen as a feint), and the possibility of another crossing around Pakokku. IV Corps' build-up opposite Nyaungu had aroused some suspicion, but not enough for the Japanese command to order a stronger defense to be set up given the widespread activity along what was a 200-mile (322km) front. However, at the last minute the commander of the *33rd Division*, concerned about the gap between his division and *28th Army*, ordered a battalion from the *215th Regiment* to be sent to the area around Nyaungu and Pagan to reinforce the Indian National Army troops guarding the area.

As soon as 114th Brigade had driven the Japanese out of Kanhla, the rest of 7th Division hurriedly moved up troops, equipment, and assault boats to the designated crossing points on the Irrawaddy. General Messervy had scheduled the crossing for the night of February 13/14, to follow on the heels of 20th Division's crossing, and there was little time to prepare. Some of the assault boats were found to have been damaged in transit, but were made ready just in time. After a final reconnaissance by detachments from the Special Boat Section and the Sea Reconnaissance Unit, at 3.45am on the morning of 14 February, a company of the 2nd Battalion, South Lancashire Regiment, set off from the west bank of the Irrawaddy to row silently to the beaches designated "B3" and "B4". The company reached its

objective without incident, and immediately seized the high ground above "B4". Then the assault began to fall apart. At 5.30am, a half hour before dawn, the battalion's remaining two companies set off in powered assault boats, while two 1st Air Commando Group UC-64s droned back and forth overhead to drown out the noise of the outboard motors. But some of the boats began to leak, and in others the outboard motors refused to start, or broke down once on the river. The Irrawaddy current proved stronger than anticipated, carrying some boats past their intended landing beaches. As the sun came up the assault boats were still on the river, and here the Japanese and INA troops caught them with a steady stream of machine gun fire, killing the two company commanders and wounding many. Under cover of tank and artillery fire, the surviving boats turned back to their starting point.

A few hours after dawn a cab rank of 1st Air Commando B-25s and P-47s arrived overhead and began bombing and strafing the area around and behind the landing beaches, while the artillery built up a steady rate of fire. The 33rd Brigade commander decided to send across his next battalion, the 4/15th Punjabis, rather than try to reorganize the South Lancashires. The engineers hurriedly repaired the boats that had returned, and at 9.45am the Punjabis set off. Tanks and self-propelled howitzers lined the west bank of the Irrawaddy to provide support. This time the assault went well. The first few boats got across without harm, and linked up with the isolated company of the South Lancashires holding the cliffs at "B4". By early afternoon the entire battalion was across, followed by the 4/1 Gurkhas and six Sherman tanks of the 116th RAC. Farther down river, a company of Sikh infantry from 89th Brigade managed to cross the river near Pagan, where they received the surrender of a company of INA troops, and sent out patrols to link

M-7 Priests of the 59th (Self-Propelled) Field Battery, 18th Artillery Regiment, fire their 105mm guns in support of 7th Division's crossing on 14 February. The 59th Field Battery later accompanied 17th Division in the drive on Meiktila. (IWM SE 3158)

A Sherman tank of the 116th Tank Regiment, Royal Armoured Corps, crosses the Irrawaddy near Nyaungu on a section of Bailey bridge. Equipment for the crossing was far from adequate, but 14th Army had a tradition of making do with what it had. (National Archives 342-FH-3A-37409-72806AC)

up with 33rd Brigade at Nyaungu. The Japanese did not have enough troops in the area to launch a counterattack, and so could not interfere with the build-up of the bridgehead. The next day a steady stream of assault boats and rafts brought over the South Lancashire battalion and elements of 89th Brigade, which took over the western and southern flanks of the bridgehead while 33rd Brigade covered the east and southeast. The two brigades kept pushing outward, and by the end of the day on 16 February had captured and cleared the village of Nyaungu and extended the bridgehead to 6,000 yards (5,460m) wide and 4,000 yards (3,640m) deep.

Anxious to speed the attack on Meiktila, Messervy did not wait for the 7th Division to complete consolidating the bridgehead. He ordered 17th Division to begin its crossing on 17 February and establish a base outside the bridgehead area. Cowan was equally eager to begin and ordered a reconnaissance force, designated "Tomcol", to cross first with the objective of pushing out beyond the bridgehead to reconnoiter the roads leading out of Nyaungu. Later that day at 17.20hrs eight "Oscars"

CROSSING THE IRRAWADDY, 14 FEBRUARY 1945

(pages 50–51)

4/15th Punjab Regiment (1) crossed the Irrawaddy River around 10.00 am on the morning of 14 February 1945. IV Corps had assigned the task of crossing the river and seizing a bridgehead to the 7th Indian Division. After careful reconnaissance, Lieutenant-General Frank Messervy, IV Corps' commander, selected a stretch of riverbank about a mile northeast of the small village of Nyaungu. The landing beaches were designated 'B4' (2), 'B3' (3), 'B2' (4), and 'B1' (out of the scene to the right). The plan called for the 2nd Battalion, South Lancashire Regiment, to make a crossing just before dawn and seize the high ground above the beaches, to be followed by the rest of 33rd Brigade. The crossing at Nyaungu took the Japanese by surprise. Unknown to IV Corps, Nyaungu was the boundary between the Japanese *15th* and *28th Armies*, and neither army had seen fit to establish firm contact with the other. At the last minute the commander of *33rd Division* ordered a battalion from *214th Regiment* sent to the area to join some units the Indian National Army assigned to guarding the river. Nevertheless, there were too few Japanese troops in the bridgehead area to mount a determined defense or launch a counterattack. In the hour before dawn one company of the South Lancashires successfully made a silent crossing and quickly seized the bluffs above 'B4' beach (5), but problems with the assault boats delayed the rest of the battalion. The assault boats (6) used in the crossing were made of wood, powered by a 9.8-horsepower outboard motor. The boats

and engines had traveled overland from Imphal over rough tracks and many were damaged en route; about half were considered to be reliable. Each boat could carry a squad of soldiers with their small arms, but no heavy weapons. A trained sapper (7) steered the boat to the beaches and back across the river. Once out on the river many of the assault boats carrying the South Lancashires broke down or were swept passed their landing sites in the strong current. As dawn broke over the river, the Japanese and Indian National Army troops on the bluffs above the river opened fire with machine-guns with devastating effect. Those boats that could, returned to their starting point and the crossing ground to a halt. While Indian Army sappers hurriedly repaired the boats, the commander of 33rd Brigade ordered the 4/15th Punjab Regiment to cross the river as soon as the boats were ready. The 1st Air Commando Group's two fighter squadrons, equipped with P-47s (8), made repeated bombing and strafing runs over the landing beaches to soften up the area for the 4/15th Punjabs and to protect the now isolated company of South Lancashires above 'B4' beach. With the sun now well up, the 7th Division's artillery moved closer to the river and opened fire. The Sherman tanks of the 114th R.A.C. joined in to add to the weight of fire. At 9.45 am the assault boats set off again with the 4/15th Punjab on board. This time the assault went off as planned. The 4/15th Punjabs landing successfully on 'B3' and 'B2' beaches, quickly linking up with the South Lancashires and rapidly pushing inland. (Howard Gerrard)

One of 17th Division's mechanized columns advancing over the dry, dusty roads to Meiktila. In all some 3,000 vehicles set out from Nyaungu in multiple columns under cover of cab-rank patrols throughout the day. (IWM SE 3071)

from the *64th Sentai* strafed the Nyaungu–Pakokku area, damaging a raft and some trucks, and shooting down an L-5 before they were intercepted by a flight of Spitfires from No. 152 Squadron, who claimed two "Oscars" damaged (later confirmed as destroyed). On the 18th, 48th Brigade began crossing the Irrawaddy, followed by 255th Tank Brigade the next day. Once across, the two brigades pushed on and set up a base at Nyaungyidaung, a village about seven miles (11km) from Nyaungu. Division headquarters and 63rd Brigade crossed on the 21st. With the bulk of his force across, Cowan was ready. Meiktila lay 82 miles (132km) away.

Cowan planned to advance on and capture Meiktila in five phases. In the first phase, 48th and 63rd Brigade with 255th Tank Brigade would capture the villages around Ngathayauk, straddling the first key crossroads on the advance route, then split up and advance on Taungtha from two directions. 48th Brigade with 9th (Royal Deccan) Horse would attack Taungtha via Kamye, while 63rd Brigade with 5th (Probyn's) Horse would first go southeast to Seiktein, then turn east to approach Taungtha via Welaung. By splitting the Division into two groups Cowan could speed the advance and, for a few days at least, conceal from the Japanese his true intentions. In the second phase, while 48th Brigade held Taungtha, 63rd Brigade would capture Mahlaing on the Taungtha–Meiktila road, where the Division would concentrate. As the third phase, Cowan planned to capture a Japanese airfield at Thabutkon, where his air-transportable 99th Brigade could be flown in. Then, in phases four and five, the Division would first cut the routes into Meiktila and isolate the town, and then attack the town directly and capture it.

The 4/12th Frontier Force Regiment advance on Seywa village, which was cleared with only light opposition. *Burma Area Army* was not yet fully aware of 17th Division's breakout. (IWM IND 4447

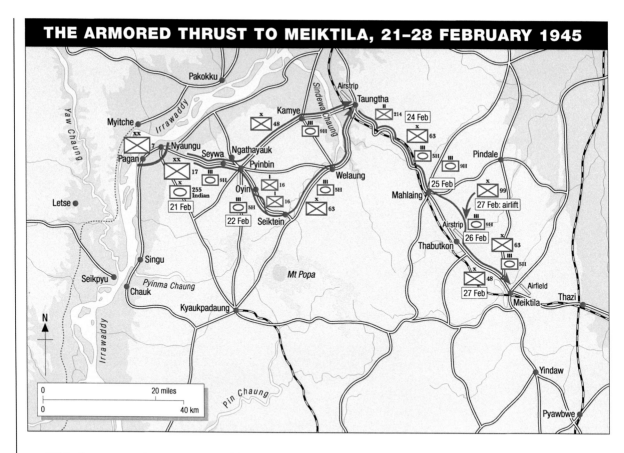

With the reconnaissance troops of "Tomcol" out in front, 17th Division began its advance to Meiktila early in the morning of 21 February with the day's objective the villages around Ngathayauk, 16 miles (26km) from Nyaungu. Within hours a column of over 3,000 vehicles was on the move. The bridgehead closed up behind the advance force; from now on 17th Division and 255th Tank Brigade would be entirely dependent on air supply. While 48th Brigade advanced down the main road to Ngathayauk, 255th Tank Brigade followed a route just to the south. At midday, 9th (Royal Deccan) Horse and its attached infantry, 4/4th Bombay Grenadiers, attacked the village of Seywa, a mile west of Ngathayauk, and cleared it against light opposition with support from 48th Brigade. With Seywa secure, 5th (Probyn's) Horse attacked Ngathayauk from the south, clearing the seven villages in the area, again meeting only light resistance. The two infantry brigades closed up and dug in for the night around Ngathayauk.

The next morning the Division split up, to approach Taungtha from two directions. With "Tomcol" in the lead, 9th (Royal Deccan) Horse, 48th Brigade, and the Division headquarters and accompanying support units headed east toward Kamye, while 63rd Brigade with 5th (Probyn's) Horse headed south toward Seiktein. En route to Seiktein 5th (Probyn's) Horse and its infantry support, 6/7th Rajputs, ran into ferocious Japanese resistance at the village of Oyin. Two companies of the *16th Infantry Regiment*, from the *2nd Division*, had hurriedly occupied the village and dug in, adapting the air raid shelters the villagers had dug underneath their houses to create some 20 bunkers, and using the hard, dry, mud wall of the

village's artificial pond as a bastion. A screen of snipers hidden in trees along the roads into the village covered the approaches. One squadron of tanks with a company of infantry came down the road leading into the village from the north, while a second squadron attacked from the east. As the tanks approached the village snipers opened up and the infantry quickly dismounted. With the tanks spraying the trees with their Browning machine guns, the infantry entered the village but were soon pinned down by machine-gun fire. The tanks moved in, firing at any bunkers they could see. Soon much of the village was on fire, and in the smoke and dust it was difficult for the tanks to identify targets or to communicate with the infantry who were under intense machine-gun fire. When the tanks moved into the village, they ran into Japanese tank-killer teams. As the squadron commander's tank moved down a hedge line, a Japanese soldier ran out from cover with a picric acid bomb and threw himself under the tank, detonating the bomb and blowing in the tank's bottom plate, fatally wounding the driver and disabling the tank. A short time later a second Japanese soldier ran out and climbed up on an advancing tank. The tank commander shut his hatch just in time and radioed the codeword "Badmash" – the signal for tank-killers. The lead tank traversed its turret and shot the Japanese soldier off the tank with its machine-gun. A third soldier dived under another tank, but the tank quickly reversed allowing a companion tank to machine-gun the attacker. There were several more individual Japanese attacks but without result. Whenever they had the opportunity the Japanese kept up a steady fire against a tank's turret. One tank commander had two periscopes shot away and 40 hits around his turret. Several times tank commanders had to dismount to coordinate infantry attacks, and near the end of the afternoon a sniper killed one of the squadron commanders while he was working with the infantry. None of the Japanese measures could stop the tanks from moving methodically through the village, blasting bunkers and gradually reducing Japanese resistance. By the end of the day the force had killed over 50 Japanese soldiers, captured two battalion guns, several machine guns, and blown up an ammunition dump.

Oyin proved to be the toughest nut to crack on the road to Taungtha. The two prongs of the advance continued on, encountering small parties of Japanese troops that had not had time to dig in. These were quickly dealt with, 63rd Brigade inflicting over 150 casualties at the village of Kaing. On the morning of 24 February, 48th Brigade launched an attack on Taungtha, with 9th (Royal Deccan) Horse in support, running into elements of the *214th Regiment* from the *33rd Division*. The Japanese had not had time to prepare any defenses, and were quickly pushed out of the town. Late in the afternoon, 63rd Brigade and 5th (Probyn's) Horse arrived at Taungtha, and the Division set out to bivouac at Mingan, some three miles (4.8km) from Taungtha down the Taungtha–Meiktila road across relatively open country. In a scene more reminiscent of the Western Desert, the entire force raced across the ground on a broad front, jeeps, tanks, and trucks crashing through the brush in a pell-mell race to their objective. While 48th Brigade remained behind for an airdrop, 63rd Brigade and 255th Tank Brigade pushed on to Mahlaing. Encountering little more than snipers, 9th (Royal Deccan) Horse and 4/4th Bombay Grenadiers cleared the main route down to Tanaunggyin, a few miles from Mahlaing. The next morning, 26 February, 5th (Probyn's) Horse and 6/7th Rajputs cleared Mahlaing, while 9th (Royal Deccan) Horse and two companies of 4/4th Bombay Grenadiers took a wide left hook across country to capture the airfield at Thabutkon in the early afternoon. When the field had been cleared of snipers, an American Aviation Engineer Company, which had accompanied 17th Division, surveyed the field and declared it ready for landing C-47s. On 27 February, two Air Commando transport squadrons began flying in 99th Brigade from Imphal, completing the airlift on 2 March. While the airlift was underway, armored car patrols advanced down the main road to Meiktila where they encountered a strong Japanese roadblock at Mile Stone 8. Two companies from 63rd Brigade, with a squadron of tanks from 5th (Probyn's) Horse, made a left hook around the block and knocked out the Japanese artillery supporting it. After an air strike by Thunderbolts from the 1st Air Commando Group, the rest of 5th Horse

A Visual Control Point (VCP) jeep and Sherman tank on the way to Thabutkon. The VCP jeeps traveled with the forward columns to call in air strikes from the Air Commando cab-ranks overhead. (National Archives 342-FH-3A-37420-72817AC)

Troops of the 1/3rd Gurkha Rifles, 99th Indian Brigade, check their equipment after flying into Thabutkon. Major-General Cowan had converted 99th Brigade to be air-transportable, with a minimum of motor vehicles, to overcome the lack of sufficient motor transport to mechanize the entire 17th Division. (National Archives 342-FH-3A-37418-72815AC)

and a battalion of infantry broke through the roadblock. That evening, advance patrols could see fires burning in Meiktila as the Japanese began destroying their supply dumps.

By now the Japanese high command was thoroughly alarmed by the growing threat to Meiktila, having ignored earlier reports of British mechanized columns. On 23 February, the chief of staff of *Southern Army* held a conference in Meiktila to discuss strategy with the chiefs of staff of *Burma Area Army, 15th Army, 28th Army,* and *33rd Army.* Much of the discussion focused on a possible counterattack across the Irrawaddy, as the chiefs of staff were ignorant of 17th Division's advance. The Japanese intelligence staff still viewed a small-scale raid on Meiktila as the most probable British move, and remained confident that the troops in Meiktila were adequate to deal with a minor raid or airborne attack. When reports began to come in of encounters with columns of British troops with tanks moving toward Taungtha they were simply ignored. No doubt 2nd Division's crossing of the Irrawaddy on 24 February added to the Japanese confusion. The capture of Thabutkon airfield came as a rude shock. General Katamura, *15th Army* commander, recommended to General Kimura that the proposed counterattack be cancelled and all effort directed to defending Meiktila. Kimura agreed, and immediately ordered *49th Division,* then in reserve, to move to Meiktila with all speed. At Meiktila, Major-General Kasuya Tomekichi, commander of No. 2 Field Transport, which had responsibility for all the transport units supporting the *15th* and *33rd Armies,* was put in charge of the defense of the town. Kasuya had approximately 2,500 administrative and line of communications troops available, and another 2,000 from various Japanese Army Air Force units, including the *52nd* and *84th Airfield*

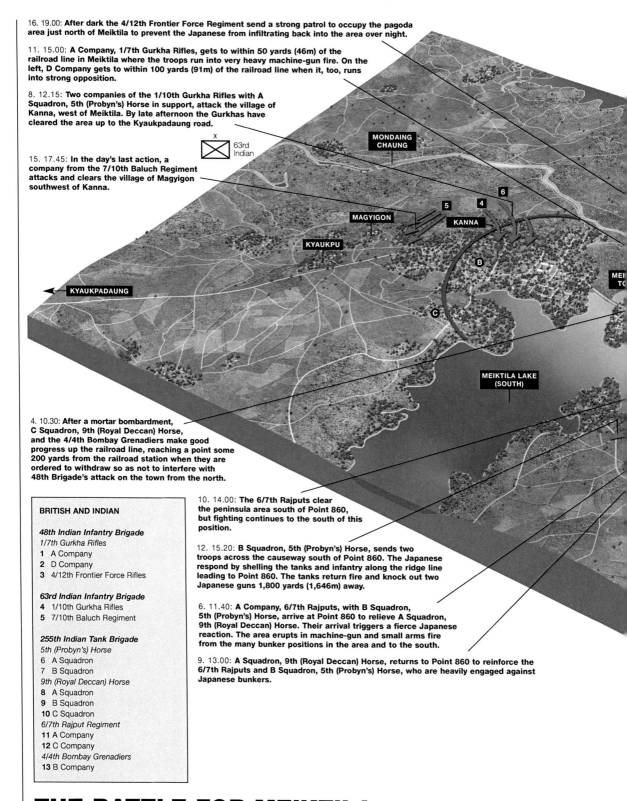

16. 19.00: After dark the 4/12th Frontier Force Regiment send a strong patrol to occupy the pagoda area just north of Meiktila to prevent the Japanese from infiltrating back into the area over night.

11. 15.00: **A Company, 1/7th Gurkha Rifles, gets to within 50 yards (46m) of the railroad line in Meiktila where the troops run into very heavy machine-gun fire. On the left, D Company gets to within 100 yards (91m) of the railroad line when it, too, runs into strong opposition.**

8. 12.15: **Two companies of the 1/10th Gurkha Rifles with A Squadron, 5th (Probyn's) Horse in support, attack the village of Kanna, west of Meiktila. By late afternoon the Gurkhas have cleared the area up to the Kyaukpadaung road.**

15. 17.45: **In the day's last action, a company from the 7/10th Baluch Regiment attacks and clears the village of Magyigon southwest of Kanna.**

x
63rd
Indian

MONDAING
CHAUNG

MAGYIGON   KANNA

KYAUKPU

KYAUKPADAUNG

B

C

MEI
TO

MEIKTILA LAKE
(SOUTH)

4. 10.30: **After a mortar bombardment, C Squadron, 9th (Royal Deccan) Horse, and the 4/4th Bombay Grenadiers make good progress up the railroad line, reaching a point some 200 yards from the railroad station when they are ordered to withdraw so as not to interfere with 48th Brigade's attack on the town from the north.**

BRITISH AND INDIAN

48th Indian Infantry Brigade
1/7th Gurkha Rifles
1 A Company
2 D Company
3 4/12th Frontier Force Rifles

63rd Indian Infantry Brigade
4 1/10th Gurkha Rifles
5 7/10th Baluch Regiment

255th Indian Tank Brigade
5th (Probyn's) Horse
6 A Squadron
7 B Squadron
9th (Royal Deccan) Horse
8 A Squadron
9 B Squadron
10 C Squadron
6/7th Rajput Regiment
11 A Company
12 C Company
4/4th Bombay Grenadiers
13 B Company

10. 14.00: **The 6/7th Rajputs clear the peninsula area south of Point 860, but fighting continues to the south of this position.**

12. 15.20: **B Squadron, 5th (Probyn's) Horse, sends two troops across the causeway south of Point 860. The Japanese respond by shelling the tanks and infantry along the ridge line leading to Point 860. The tanks return fire and knock out two Japanese guns 1,800 yards (1,646m) away.**

6. 11.40: **A Company, 6/7th Rajputs, with B Squadron, 5th (Probyn's) Horse, arrive at Point 860 to relieve A Squadron, 9th (Royal Deccan) Horse. Their arrival triggers a fierce Japanese reaction. The area erupts in machine-gun and small arms fire from the many bunker positions in the area and to the south.**

9. 13.00: **A Squadron, 9th (Royal Deccan) Horse, returns to Point 860 to reinforce the 6/7th Rajputs and B Squadron, 5th (Probyn's) Horse, who are heavily engaged against Japanese bunkers.**

THE BATTLE FOR MEIKTILA

1 March 1945, viewed from the south, showing the attacks on Meiktila town and the attempts to overwhelm the Japanese garrison by 48th Brigade, 63rd Brigade, and 255th Tank Brigade.

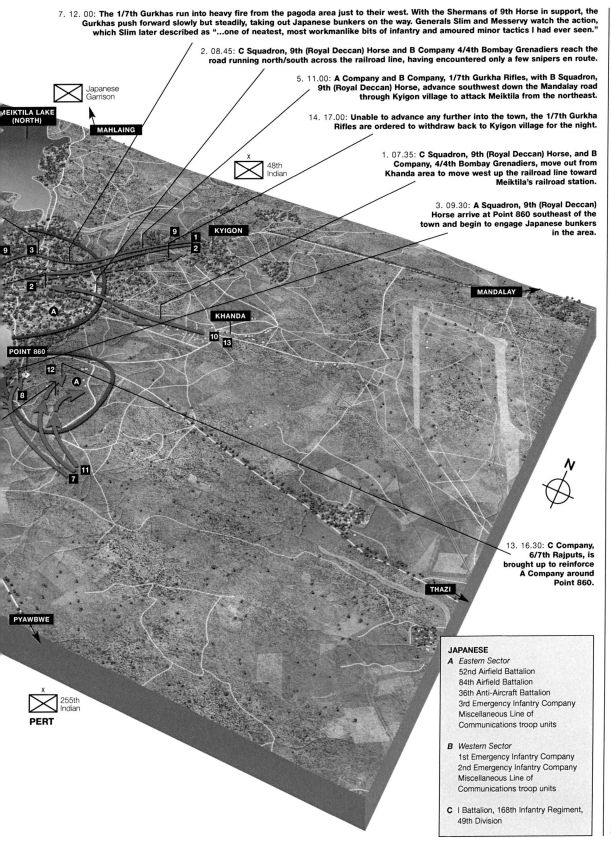

7. 12. 00: The 1/7th Gurkhas run into heavy fire from the pagoda area just to their west. With the Shermans of 9th Horse in support, the Gurkhas push forward slowly but steadily, taking out Japanese bunkers on the way. Generals Slim and Messervy watch the action, which Slim later described as "...one of neatest, most workmanlike bits of infantry and amoured minor tactics I had ever seen."

2. 08.45: C Squadron, 9th (Royal Deccan) Horse and B Company 4/4th Bombay Grenadiers reach the road running north/south across the railroad line, having encountered only a few snipers en route.

5. 11.00: A Company and B Company, 1/7th Gurkha Rifles, with B Squadron, 9th (Royal Deccan) Horse, advance southwest down the Mandalay road through Kyigon village to attack Meiktila from the northeast.

14. 17.00: Unable to advance any further into the town, the 1/7th Gurkha Rifles are ordered to withdraw back to Kyigon village for the night.

1. 07.35: C Squadron, 9th (Royal Deccan) Horse, and B Company, 4/4th Bombay Grenadiers, move out from Khanda area to move west up the railroad line toward Meiktila's railroad station.

3. 09.30: A Squadron, 9th (Royal Deccan) Horse arrive at Point 860 southeast of the town and begin to engage Japanese bunkers in the area.

Japanese Garrison

MEIKTILA LAKE (NORTH)

MAHLAING

x 48th Indian

KYIGON

MANDALAY

KHANDA

POINT 860

THAZI

13. 16.30: C Company, 6/7th Rajputs, is brought up to reinforce A Company around Point 860.

PYAWBWE

x 255th Indian

PERT

JAPANESE

A *Eastern Sector*
52nd Airfield Battalion
84th Airfield Battalion
36th Anti-Aircraft Battalion
3rd Emergency Infantry Company
Miscellaneous Line of
Communications troop units

B *Western Sector*
1st Emergency Infantry Company
2nd Emergency Infantry Company
Miscellaneous Line of
Communications troop units

C I Battalion, 168th Infantry Regiment,
49th Division

Battalions and the *36th Anti-Aircraft Battalion.* The administrative and line of communications troops were hastily organized into three emergency infantry companies and a mobile reserve force. Any hospital patient who could walk or shoot was sent out to man a bunker. Kasuya set up a western and eastern sector for the defense of the town, with the dividing line being Meiktila's northern and southern artificial lakes. The troops in Meiktila hurriedly prepared bunkers throughout the town and laid mines and booby traps along the approaches. Kasuya opened up the ordnance depots around the town and ensured that all units were well supplied with medium and light machine guns, and had plenty of ammunition.

A 3.7in. howitzer of the 6th Jacob's Mountain Artillery Battery fires in support of the attack on Meiktila. (IWM IND 4601)

At the last minute, *I Battalion, 168th Infantry Regiment* arrived from *49th Division* and was hastily sent to occupy positions in the western section of Meiktila. The regimental commander and some additional troops reached the town just before the approaches were cut.

Cowan was now ready for the next phase of his attack, the isolation of Meiktila. His plan was to have 63rd Brigade attack from the west, 48th Brigade to attack from the north down the Mahlaing–Meiktila road, and for 255th Tank Brigade to make a wide flanking movement north of the town to attack from the east. On the morning of 28 February the three brigades set out. Leaving its transport behind, and placing one battalion with the divisional artillery, 63rd Brigade set out on foot toward the western edge of the town. After an air strike nearby, the divisional artillery established a base at the village of Antu, where it could cover all sectors of the attack. By the end of the day 63rd Brigade had set up a base at Kyaukpyugon, and established a roadblock southwest of Meiktila on the road to Kyaukpadaung. Patrols probed the approaches to the town and found them well defended. To the north, 48th Brigade pushed down the Mahlaing–Meiktila road until it reached a bridge over a *chaung* about a mile from the town where the forward units ran into heavy machine-gun fire. Two companies pushed across the *chaung*, but then pulled back due to the approaching darkness. That night, 48th Brigade sent out patrols to probe the approaches to Meiktila, but these patrols ran into intense fire from a pagoda complex guarding the road leading into town.

The bulk of the fighting that day took place on the eastern approaches to the town. Around mid-morning 255th Tank Brigade set out on its wide sweep around Meiktila. The Brigade sent two recce columns ahead, each composed of a squadron of tanks from 9th (Royal Deccan) Horse, armored cars from 16th Cavalry, infantry, and a Valentine bridging tank. On reaching the Mandalay–Meiktila road "A" Group turned east and followed the road to the village of Kyigon, about two miles from Meiktila, without meeting any opposition. "B" Group went past the road and turned east to sweep across the main Meiktila airfield. They did not encounter any opposition until they had crossed the railway line at Khanda, where the group ran into heavy artillery, machine-gun, and sniper fire. This came from the area east and south of a canal that ran parallel to the railway, which formed a natural tank trap. The ground to the east and south of the

railway line was difficult, with scrub brush, and many trees and houses providing the Japanese defenders with good cover. 5th (Probyn's) Horse and the 6/7th Rajputs came in right behind "B" Group and deployed for an attack, but the infantry on the left flank began to take heavy casualties. The squadron commander on that flank moved his tank troops forward in support, but found that the Japanese were setting fire to petrol tanks all around him. When he opened his turret to see what was happening, he was shot in the head. The Brigade then ordered the 9th (Royal Deccan) Horse's squadron to move up to a ridgeline that bordered the southern lake near Point 860, in the hope that the tanks could provide covering fire. This squadron destroyed a number of bunkers, but as it was late in the day and the infantry could still not go forward, the entire attack was called off and the tanks returned to base around Khanda.

1 March saw the bitterest fighting of the three-day battle for Meiktila as Cowan's three brigades forced their way into the town against tenacious

FIGHTING IN MEIKTILA, 1 MARCH 1945 (pages 62–63)
The attack on Meiktila began on 28 February 1945 with the 48th Brigade attacking the town from the north and the 63rd Brigade attacking from the west, while the 255th Tank Brigade made a wide sweep around the town to attack from the east. The Japanese commander assigned to defend the town had hurriedly organized the line of communications and Japanese Army Air Force units in the surrounding area into emergency infantry companies. While not trained infantry, these soldiers (1) still fought tenaciously; few surrendered. Equipped with the Model 99 7.7mm rifle, the Japanese troops defending the town also had a plentiful supply of medium and light machine-guns and copious amounts of ammunition. The Japanese built bunkers underneath houses and in buildings throughout the town, and set up anti-tank and field guns to defend against the tanks. On 1 March, 48th Brigade began to push into the center of town from the northeast. By this time artillery fire and air strikes had destroyed or damaged many of the buildings in the town (2). That day 'A' and 'D' Companies of the the 1/7th Gurkha Rifles led the attack, with support from two troops of Sherman tanks of the 9th (Royal Deccan) Horse. The attack began at 11.00 am. With the help of the Royal Deccan's tanks, the Gurkhas pushed slowly into the town, taking out a bunker complex around a pagoda just outside the town with grenades and the Sherman's 75mm cannon under the gaze of General William Slim and LtGen Frank Messervy who flew in that day to view the fighting. Once inside the town the troops moved forward in short rushes toward their objective, the Railway Station, pausing after each rush to lay down fire before their next run (3). The troops had to keep a constant look out for the many snipers that lurked in the burned-out buildings (4) As the afternoon wore on, the Gurkhas ran into very heavy machine-gun fire that slowed their progress. The Japanese had planted real and dummy mines along the streets in town, preventing the tanks from moving forward until the mines could be cleared. Sappers moved forward to lift the mines, but came under continuous sniper fire and were unable to clear the streets for the tanks. The Gurkhas kept up a steady stream of fire against any positions they could see (5), with the tanks firing from a distance, inflicting heavy casualties among the Japanese. By the end of the afternoon the forward Gurkha units had reached a point some 50 yards from the Railway Station, but could get no farther without the tanks. At 5.00 pm the Gurkhas were ordered to withdraw back to their night positions outside the town. (Howard Gerrard)

opposition. It was a slow, methodical process of winkling the Japanese from every bunker and every house, under constant sniping, in the intense heat of the Burmese dry season. As Meiktila was a large town, it contained many brick houses and pagodas as well as the wooden *bashas* found in all Burmese villages. Many contained bunkers, often dug under the corner of the house, which were difficult to see. Each house or pagoda had to be checked and cleared, and each bunker destroyed. Early in the morning the 9th (Royal Deccan) Horse sent two squadrons of tanks to support 48th Brigade's advance, while a squadron from 5th (Probyn's) Horse joined up with 63rd Brigade. Then the Air Commandos put in a series of air strikes around the town, followed by an artillery bombardment. To the north, 48th Brigade shifted its approach and sent the 1/7 Gurkha Rifles to attack down the Mandalay–Meiktila road. The Gurkhas cleared Kyigon, and advanced into Meiktila town, getting to within 100 yards (91m) of the railroad line before the attack was called off in the late afternoon. The Japanese had laid dummy minefields along the way, covering bricks to make them look like mines, but had also placed aerial bombs as improvised anti-tank mines. Both slowed down the pace of the advance, as did the very heavy volume of machine-gun fire. In the eastern sector, 255th Tank Brigade retook Point 860 with tanks from 5th (Probyn's) and 9th (Royal Deccan) Horse and the 6/7th Rajputs. When the infantry reached the position and dismounted from the tanks, they immediately came under heavy sniper fire from camouflaged bunkers all around the ridgeline. These had to be taken out one by one. Rather than attack through the area of rough ground assaulted the day before, the Brigade sent a mixed force of 9th (Royal Deccan) Horse tanks and 4/4th Bombay Grenadiers down the railroad line toward the town, probing the Japanese defenses. This force got to within 200 yards (182m) of the railroad station when it was ordered to withdraw so as not to run into 48th Brigade's attack. In the western sector, 63rd Brigade cleared the village of Khanna and then pushed on past the village to clear the railroad line and the main Kyaukpadaung–Meiktila road. The tanks moved with the infantry, blasting bunkers along the way. General Slim and General Messervy chose this day

A P-47D of the 5th Fighter Squadron, 1st Air Commando Group, armed with two 500lb bombs and a drop tank in preparation for a cab-rank patrol. (Author's collection)

to visit Cowan and witness the battle first-hand. In his memoirs, Slim wrote of Cowan, "To watch a highly skilled, experienced, and resolute commander controlling a hard-fought battle is to see, not only a man triumphing over the highest mental and physical stresses, but an artist producing his effects in the most complicated and difficult of all the arts."

The next day the Division drew the ring around Meiktila even tighter. In the north, 48th Brigade resumed its advance, with the 4/12th Frontier Force Regiment in the lead. The Japanese had infiltrated back into the positions they had been forced to abandon the day before, and had to be pushed out all over again. Under heavy machine-gun and sniper fire the infantry and tanks had advanced to within 50 yards (46m) of the railroad line by mid-morning when a 75mm gun knocked out one of 9th (Royal Deccan)

Major-General Cowan discussing the attack with Brigadier Hedley, CO of 48th Indian Brigade, outside Meiktila. (IWM SE 3275)

Horse's tanks on the right flank at close range. A few minutes later a gun took out another tank, and then a third on the left flank of the attack. The range was so close that the accompanying infantry saw the gun's muzzle flash and killed the gun crew with rifle and machine-gun fire. At the end of the day the Brigade pulled back to the pagoda area. In the western sector, 63rd Brigade cleared the eastern section of Khanna, and pushed down the main road toward Meiktila, reaching the causeway that linked the western and eastern sides of the town. As the 5th (Probyn's) Horse squadron commander reached the causeway, his tank and the tank of one of his troop commanders received direct hits from a 75mm gun firing from the opposite end, but fortunately the damage was minimal. The infantry and tanks then pushed south toward the village of Kyaukpu to clear the area along the south lake. As the tanks entered a belt of thick scrub ahead of the infantry, Japanese tank killer teams attacked the tanks with mines and petrol bombs. One tank had its track disabled, but the other tanks in the troop managed to kill the assault teams with their machine guns before more damage could be done. The tanks continued on, blasting any bunkers they could see and using their machine-guns to knock out snipers from the surrounding trees. When they came out of the belt of scrub, they caught the Japanese withdrawing and inflicted many casualties. In the fighting that afternoon Naik Fazal Din of the 7/10th Baluch Regiment won a posthumous Victoria Cross while leading his section in an attack on Japanese bunkers. Attacking Naik Fazal Din's section, a Japanese officer stabbed Fazal Din with his sword. Grievously wounded, Fazal Din wrenched the sword from the officer, killed him and two more Japanese soldiers attacking his section, and then urged his section to continue the attack before collapsing from his wound.

On the final day of the battle, 3 March, the three brigades concentrated on eliminating the last remaining Japanese troops in and around Meiktila. The heaviest fighting took place in the town itself and in the eastern sector. The 1st Battalion, West Yorkshire Regiment, from 48th Brigade put in the final attack with A and C Squadrons from 9th (Royal Deccan) Horse in support. A Squadron with one company of infantry came down from the north and moved up to the railroad line against light opposition. Then, after an air strike and artillery preparation, C Squadron and an infantry company attacked from the northeast against fierce opposition. A third infantry company was brought in to the attack, and in the early afternoon the tanks of A Squadron and the infantry advanced across the railroad line into the town. Heavy sniper and machine-gun fire seemed to come from every building, and as the infantry and tanks closed in on the center of town they came under fire from 75mm and anti-tank guns firing at pointblank range. A Squadron lost one tank to guns, while C Squadron lost a tank to a tank killer team, who managed to throw a grenade into the tank, killing the crew. A third tank was disabled when a mine blew off a track. Slowly and methodically the Japanese strongpoints were taken out one after another. By the end of the day the town had been cleared, and 12 enemy guns had been captured or destroyed. During the fighting Lieutenant W.B. Weston, seconded to the West Yorks from the Green Howards, was leading a platoon clearing an area of bunkers. At the last bunker Weston was badly wounded and fell in the entrance. To save his platoon from taking additional casualties, Weston took out a grenade and set it off, killing himself and the Japanese soldiers in the bunker. For his selfless sacrifice Weston was awarded a posthumous Victoria Cross, the second of the battle for Meiktila.

During the day 63rd Brigade and 255th Brigade sent out infantry and tank patrols to deal with small remaining pockets of resistance and parties of stragglers around the outskirts of the town. While it took another few days to clear out all the snipers from the area, by the end of 3 March the capture of Meiktila was complete. In the fighting for the town 17th Division had killed an estimated 2,000 Japanese soldiers and had captured some 47 field pieces and anti-tank guns, as well as the supply dumps around the town, which were promptly destroyed – a loss the Japanese could ill-afford. Many of the Japanese troops in Meiktila, including Major-General Kasuya, had managed to slip away in the night.

An Indian patrol moves through Meiktila shortly after the battle. Every house and every pile of rubble was a potential bunker. (IWM SE 3285)

14th Army now sat astride the lines of communications to *15th* and *33rd Armies* and, more critically, astride their lines of retreat to southern Burma. Cowan knew that the Japanese would make every effort to wrest Meiktila from 14th Army's grasp. Having captured Meiktila, his next task was to defend it.

THE DEFENSE OF MEIKTILA

By the first week of March General Slim had achieved his objective of forcing the Japanese to give battle. The trap he had set was now in place and his two Corps were heavily engaged along a front of some 120 miles. Success in smashing *Burma Area Army* depended on the ability of IV Corps to retain its grip on Meiktila and the routes to the south, to give time for XXXIII Corps to destroy the Japanese forces in and around the Irrawaddy bend. The objectives for IV Corps were straightforward; 17th Division had to defend Meiktila, while 7th Division had to maintain its hold on 14th Army's right flank, ensuring that the west bank of the Irrawaddy was secure and, at the right time, re-opening the road to Meiktila, which was now entirely cutoff. Within XXXIII Corps, 19th Division was about to begin the final phase of the advance to Mandalay, while 2nd Division and 20th Division, after intense fighting to expand their bridgeheads, were pushing east to attack the approaches to Mandalay from the south. To re-enforce Cowan at Meiktila, Slim decided to fly in 9th Indian Infantry Brigade (which had been converted to an air-transportable brigade) from 5th Indian Infantry Division, 14th Army's reserve division, while the rest of the Division moved closer to the front to prepare for the advance to Rangoon. In the midst of the battle, with five of his divisions across the Irrawaddy, Slim learned during the last week of February that Generalissimo Chiang Kai-shek had requested the return of all American and Chinese forces in the Northern Combat Area Command to prepare for a major offensive in China in the summer. Slim had planned that the N.C.A.C. forces would guard his left flank and tie down the Japanese in that sector; now they would be free to move south. More critically, the transfer would divert the USAAF air transport squadrons from supplying 14th Army, which would have been a disaster. Despite every effort to build up land or river-based lines of communications, at this point in the campaign Slim's divisions were almost entirely dependent on air supply. Mountbatten appealed directly to the Combined Chiefs of Staff, and the American Joint Chiefs ultimately agreed that the American transport squadrons would not leave Burma until the capture of Rangoon or 1 June, whichever came first. This came as a great relief to Slim, but he and his commanders were now under even greater pressure to get to Rangoon.

After the capture of Meiktila, *Burma Area Army* gave up any idea of launching a counteroffensive across the Irrawaddy. The objective now was to stabilize the situation. But for *15th* and *33rd Armies* to hold the British along the Irrawaddy, Meiktila had to be retaken. General Kimura believed this could be done. He had already sent *49th Division* north toward Meiktila. Earlier in February, at the request of General Katamura, General Kimura had agreed to transfer the *18th Division*, less one regiment left fighting the Chinese, from *33rd Army* to *15th Army* to provide support for the coming battles around Mandalay. Just before

Meiktila's fall Kimura ordered *18th Division* to Meiktila to defend the
town. When the town fell, Kimura then ordered *18th Division* to
coordinate with *49th Division* to retake the town. General Katamura
agreed to reinforce *18th Division* with units from *15th Army*. He ordered
the *119th Infantry Regiment* from *53rd Division* to Pindale to cover
18th Division, and transferred two battalions of the *214th Infantry
Regiment* from *33rd Division* (designated the "*Sakuma Force*") directly to
18th Division's control. The *Sakuma Force* was ordered to approach
Meiktila from the west, down the Mahlaing–Meiktila road, to block the
British escape route back to the Irrawaddy. Katamura then transferred
the bulk of *15th Army's* heavy artillery to *18th Division*, under a Colonel
Naganuma. The "*Naganuma Force*" consisted of two Model 96 150mm
howitzers, nine Model 92 105mm howitzers, 21 Model 41 and Model 90
75mm guns, and 13 anti-tank guns. The heavy guns moved up to an
area near Myindawgan Lake where they were in a position to shell
Meiktila town and the airfield. Lastly, Katamura assigned the *14th Tank
Regiment* to *18th Division*, though by this date the regiment had
been reduced to a mere nine tanks. Katamura's plan was to have
214th Regiment advance on Meiktila from the west, while *18th Division*
came in from the north. He instructed *18th Division* to coordinate its
attacks with *49th Division* coming up from the south.

General Cowan expected the Japanese to use every effort to dislodge
17th Division from Meiktila, and he made immediate preparations for
its defense. After the capture of the town, the infantry brigades spent
the next few days clearing the area around Meiktila of any remaining
snipers and Japanese stragglers. Cowan divided the town into sectors,
and assigned a brigade to each sector. Divisional infantry held the eastern
part of the town, with Division artillery and 48th Brigade holding the sector
along the eastern side of the south lake. 63rd Brigade held Meiktila's
western section, with 255th Tank Brigade holding the western side of the
south lake. Within each sector Cowan set up a heavily defended "redoubt",
manned by an infantry company with a plentiful supply of machine guns
and anti-tank guns. With the airfield at Meiktila now open, Cowan shut
down the airfield at Thabutkon and pulled 99th Brigade back to the area
around Kyigon, and charged it with defense of the town and Meiktila's
airfield. From patrols and intelligence reports Cowan knew that the **69**

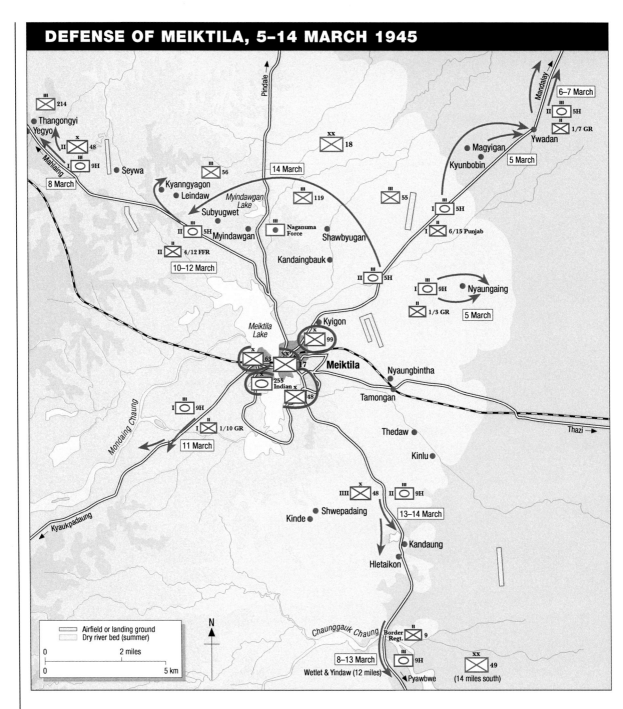

Japanese were approaching Meiktila from several directions. He chose a strategy of aggressive defense. Rather than wait to be attacked, Cowan planned on sending out strong mobile columns of tanks and infantry, with artillery and VCP support, to disrupt the Japanese before they could concentrate. He intended to ensure that 17th Division maintained the initiative. He was confident that 17th Division could hold the town. He had strong air support from the Air Commando and RAF fighter squadrons, and the relatively dry and open country around Meiktila gave his tanks an advantage.

Troops and supplies flying to Meiktila. Throughout most of the battle, 17th Division was totally reliant on air transport for all its supplies and fuel. (National Archives 342-FH-3A-3784-72751AC)

Following Japanese Army tactical doctrine of seeking quick results with the forces at hand, the commander of *18th Division* decided not to wait for *49th Division* to arrive from the south before he began his own attacks on Meiktila. But with insufficient motor transport and Allied air superiority over the battlefield during the day, it took time for *18th Division's* units to assemble in the area around Meiktila. This gave Cowan's columns the opportunity to disrupt the Japanese formations as they neared Meiktila and prepared for their own probing attacks against the town's defenses. Cowan sent out his first sweeps as soon as Meiktila had been secured. The armored cars of 11th Cavalry (P.A.V.O.) and 16th Cavalry were constantly patrolling the approaches to Meiktila or pushing out ahead of the tank and infantry columns searching for any signs of Japanese troops. When information came in that a Japanese force was concentrating on the Meiktila–Mandalay road around the Ywadan area, Cowan ordered a tank and infantry force to clear the area. A squadron from 5th (Probyn's) Horse with infantry, armored cars, and a mountain artillery battery set out early on the morning of 5 March. After dropping off the mountain battery at a British roadblock to cover the advance, the tanks and infantry set out cross-country parallel to the main road. At a village near Ywadan a 75mm gun opened fire on the leading tanks, and soon three other guns had opened fire. The VCP called in an air strike, with the tanks marking the target with high explosive shells. As the tanks and infantry approached the position, two 75mm shells hit one tank disabling it, though the crew kept firing using manual control. In the fighting that followed the tanks and infantry killed an estimated 180

Having dismounted from the tanks, the infantry move forward to clear the area of any Japanese troops. (IWM SE 3095)

Japanese soldiers and captured four 75mm guns. Meanwhile, an armored car patrol from the 11th Cavalry (P.A.V.O.) had pushed further up the road and destroyed a Japanese tankette and captured a 105mm gun.

The next day Cowan sent five columns of tanks, infantry, and artillery out from Meiktila to sweep the main roads leading to Mahlaing, Kyaukpadaung, Pyawbwe, Thazi, and Mandalay. These patrols ran into small groups of Japanese, inflicting a number of casualties. On 7 March, the patrols went out again, searching for Japanese movements. A company of infantry from 48th Brigade patrolling down the road to Pyawbwe with armored cars ran into strong opposition from elements of *49th Division* around Mile Stone 319, where a 75mm gun knocked out one armored car. A second

General Slim speaking to British and Indian troops of 17th Division at Meiktila. (IWM SE 3673)

patrol moving up the road to Mahlaing learned from local villagers that the Japanese were infiltrating the area during the night. This intelligence led to a strong response the following day, 8 March. A column from 48th Brigade with one squadron of tanks from 9th (Royal Deccan) Horse, accompanied by a battery of mountain artillery, pushed up the Mahlaing–Meiktila road. Near the villages of Thangongyi and Yego, 10 miles (16km) from Meiktila, the force ran into enemy positions and artillery belonging to the *214th Regiment.* The tanks caught several parties of Japanese troops in the open, and inflicted heavy casualties, also destroying two 105mm guns and a 75mm gun. Another strong column, consisting of two companies from the 9th Battalion, Border Regiment from 63rd Brigade, with tanks from 9th (Royal Deccan) Horse, armored cars, and artillery, headed south to clear the Japanese block on the road to Pyawbwe. Near the village of Wetlet the force came under mortar and artillery fire from the *106th Infantry Regiment,* in its first engagement. One

A Humber armored car of the 16th Light Cavalry patrols the approaches to Meiktila. The armored cars were constantly active, searching for any signs of a Japanese build-up. (IWM IND 4455)

Indian infantry riding out on Sherman tanks. Major-General Cowan kept up an aggressive defense of Meiktila using strong armored columns of tanks, infantry, and artillery to strike at the Japanese before they could concentrate for an attack. (IWM SE 3486)

Checking a bomb shelter near a house in the village. Many Burmese families built a bomb shelter under or next to their houses, which the Japanese converted into fortified bunkers. The dry season heat baked the earth hard, giving added protection (IWM SE3108).

of the regiment's 75mm guns knocked out an armored car. Two platoons went into the village with a troop of tanks, clearing the Japanese from the village and knocking out the 75mm gun. Two more guns were captured, but a tank had a track blown off by a mine and had to be abandoned. Late in the afternoon as the force withdrew north to laager around Yindaw, another tank was hit by a hollow-charge shell from a 75mm gun and burnt out. The 63rd Brigade commander decided to send additional infantry and tanks out the next day, and the combined force spent two days clearing the area. For the infantry, this meant moving through stands of trees and in and around *bashas*, looking for bunkers, clearing them with a few hand grenades and a burst of fire through the rear entrance, then moving on to the next line, always alert for snipers. In the three days of fighting, the Border Regiment suffered 141 casualties, the Japanese losing some 300 troops killed in action, and several regimental guns.

Heavy fighting continued for several days northwest of Meiktila as the *214th Regiment* and the newly arrived *56th Infantry Regiment*, probing for an opening into the town from the west, ran into British infantry and tank patrols. On 10 March, 17th Division sent a force of armored cars, infantry, and tanks from 5th (Probyn's) Horse up the road to Mahlaing to escort some of the Division's B echelon back to Meiktila. The force ran into Japanese troops and 75mm guns entrenched on both sides of the road at Mile Stone $5^{1}/_{2}$. Two troops of tanks moved around the right flank of the Japanese position and cleared much of it, moving on to clear the village of Leindaw, where they destroyed a 75mm gun and a 37mm anti-tank gun. For the next two days infantry and tanks continued clearing the area around Leindaw and Kyanngyagon, the *214th Regiment* and the *56th Regiment* both suffering heavily and losing several guns. During the fighting the British force repeatedly came under heavy artillery fire from 75mm and 105mm guns that appeared to be located around the Pindale–Meiktila road south of Myindawgan Lake, which prompted 17th Division to send two squadrons from 5th (Probyn's) Horse on an armored sweep around the area north of Meiktila on the 14th. The sweep started out moving up the road to Mandalay, then turned and headed west to cross the Pindale road, then proceeded to the Mahlaing–Meiktila road north of Leindaw. By the end of the day the sweep had netted two 105mm guns, three 75mm guns, and a 47mm anti-tank gun.

On 13 March two squadrons from 9th (Royal Deccan) Horse escorted a force of four infantry companies from 48th Brigade down the Meiktila–Pyawbwe road to Kandaung,

CLEARING WETLET, 8 MARCH 1945 (pages 74–75)

Having lost Meiktila to the 17th Division's rapid attack, the Japanese were determined to regain it. General Kimura, commander of *Burma Area Army*, ordered the *18th Division* and the *49th Division*, with reinforcements, to retake the town. But with complete Allied air superiority over the battlefield, movement by day was hazardous, and with a limited number of trucks restricted to traveling at night it took some time for the two Japanese divisions to move to Meiktila. Following Japanese tactical doctrine, the Japanese sent units into the attack as soon as they had arrived rather than waiting to concentrate for an attack in greater strength. This worked to the advantage of the 17th Division, which was then able to attack and disrupt the Japanese before they could marshal a stronger force. Major-General Cowan, the 17th Division's commander, was determined to retain the initiative and adopted an aggressive defense, using his superiority in tanks, mechanized infantry, and air power to attack the Japanese wherever they could be found. Cowan routinely sent out strong mobile columns of tanks, infantry, and artillery on sweeps around Meiktila. On 8 March, the 63rd Brigade sent out 'A' and 'B' companies from the 9th Battalion, the Border Regiment, with two troops of Sherman tanks from the 9th (Royal Deccan) Horse and a mountain artillery battery in support. They were to conduct a reconnaissance in force towards Pyawbwe, southeast of Meiktila. Japanese troops with artillery were reported in the village of Wetlet. Around noon the attack on the village (1) began. The Shermans (2) moved forward with the infantry. Communication between the tanks and the infantry was never easy, particularly in the heat and noise of battle. The tank commanders (3) often had to keep their heads out of their turrets in order to identify targets, a dangerous practice when snipers were present, as they usually were. The infantry would advance in a line (4), keeping a sharp lookout for snipers and any signs of Japanese bunkers. The Burmese villagers would often build air raid shelters under or next to their houses (5), which the Japanese soldiers would convert into machine gun bunkers. When the infantry could locate a bunker, the Shermans would be called in to blast it with their 75mm cannon (6). The tanks provided suppressing fire with their machine guns to allow the infantry to move forward, who would use their No.4 rifles (7) and Bren guns (8) to clear a village of any Japanese troops they encountered. That day 'A' Company encountered a nest of bunkers in a wooded area to the left of the village and met with sniper and mortar fire as they closed on the wood. Two platoons cleared the woods around the village while a third platoon entered the village with the tanks, capturing one gun and knocking out a second. By 4.00 pm the village had been cleared, with one 37mm anti-tank gun and one 75mm field gun captured and two more anti-tank guns knocked out. The Japanese, from the *106th Infantry Regiment*, lost over 100 killed, many by the tanks, while the Borderers lost 4 killed and 28 wounded in the action. (Howard Gerrard)

Re-supplying a Sherman tank of the 5th (Probyn's) Horse with 75mm rounds and .30 caliber ammunition after a patrol. At the end of a sweep the tanks would return to a defended base in or around Meiktila for re-supply and maintenance. (IWM IND 4640)

running into the *III Battalion, 106th Regiment*, moving up from Pyawbwe. When a patrol was fired on from Hletaikon, the next village, two companies attacked with the tanks in support, encountering what the 9th Horse called "fanatical opposition" from troops in bunkers and snipers. Clearing the village took all afternoon with the tanks heavily engaged in coordinated attacks with the infantry. In heavy fighting that day and the next, the *III Battalion* lost 300 soldiers killed in action, as well as two 70mm mountain guns and a 37mm anti-tank gun. The 48th Brigade force returned to base on the 15th.

To date the *18th Division* had little to show for its efforts. None of its regiments had managed to open a route into Meiktila from the west or the north. After nearly a week of fighting, Cowan still held the initiative. While the Japanese were able to infiltrate back into an area once the British tanks and infantry withdrew, they could not stop them from coming back. The tanks were causing heavy casualties, particularly in guns. Far too few tanks had been knocked out. The Division had to find another way to get the British out of Meiktila. From his headquarters north of the town, the division commander could see the steady stream of transport aircraft flying in and out of Meiktila's airfield. The Japanese decided to switch the focus of their assault to the main airfield: cut off the flow of supplies, and the British would be starved out of Meiktila. At the same time, General Kimura realized that he needed to re-organize the Japanese effort to retake the town. The situation along the Irrawaddy was now desperate. By 12 March, 19th Division had captured Mandalay Hill and was battering at Fort Dufferin inside Mandalay. South of Mandalay 2nd Division was close to capturing Ava, while 20th Division was pushing steadily east to cut off the routes from Mandalay to the south. General Katamura, *15th Army* commander, was too preoccupied with the battles along the Irrawaddy to control the battle for Meiktila at the same time. On 14 March, Kimura ordered *33rd Army* to take over responsibility for the fighting at Meiktila. He gave General Honda control over *18th Division, 49th Division,* and *53rd Division* then at Taungtha. He then gave *18th Division* direct control

A section of 2nd Division troops moving past a Japanese bunker position south of Mandalay. (IWM SE 3114)

15. 28–29 MARCH: **63rd Brigade advances east from the north bank of Meiktila Lake toward the Pindale road. The Brigade makes good progress and on 29 March turns south to link up with 99th Brigade moving north.**

14. 27–28 MARCH: **99th Brigade continue to push north of the sluice running into Meiktila Lake north of the town, but run into heavy machine-gun fire.**

11. 23–24 MARCH: **During the night of 23 March,** *49th Division* launches a major attack on Meiktila. The *106th Infantry Regiment* sends two battalions to attack 48th Brigade's defensive box southeast of the town. The attack is beaten back with heavy losses.

XX
17th
Indian
COWAN

MONDAING CHAUNG

MEIKTILA LAKE (SOUTH)

7

4

3

1

H

SHWEPADAING

I

3

9

9. 21–22 MARCH: **Countering a build-up by** *49th Division* **southeast of Meiktila, 48th Brigade and 9th (Royal Deccan) Horse engage the** *168th Infantry Regiment* **around Shwepadaing.**

8. 20 MARCH: *55th Infantry Regiment* **and** *119th Infantry Regiment* **with a few tanks from** *14th Tank Regiment* **attack the airfield and 99th Brigade's defensive box around Kyigon, but are beaten back.**

G

3. 15 MARCH: **9th Indian Infantry Brigade, 5th Indian Division, begins flying into Meiktila to reinforce 17th Division, despite the intermittent shelling.**

PYAWBWE

N

XX
49th
TAKEHARA

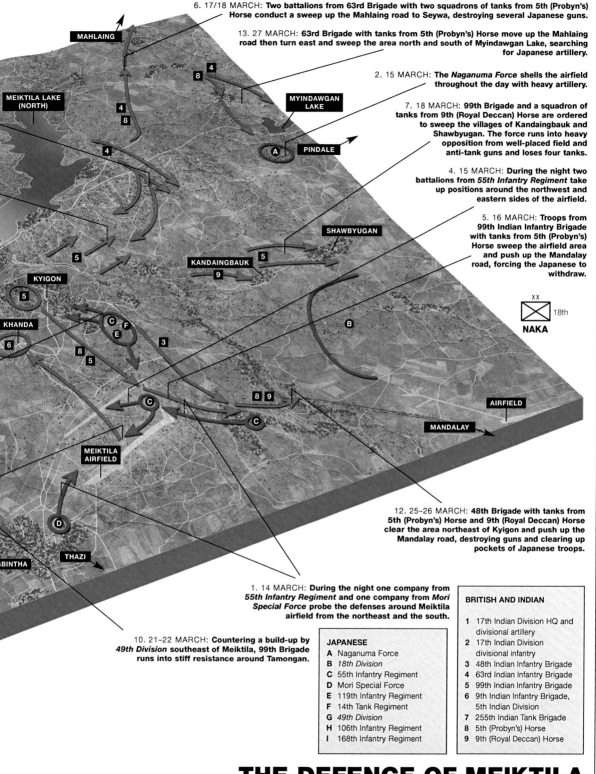

6. 17/18 MARCH: Two battalions from 63rd Brigade with two squadrons of tanks from 5th (Probyn's) Horse conduct a sweep up the Mahlaing road to Seywa, destroying several Japanese guns.

13. 27 MARCH: 63rd Brigade with tanks from 5th (Probyn's) Horse move up the Mahlaing road then turn east and sweep the area north and south of Myindawgan Lake, searching for Japanese artillery.

2. 15 MARCH: The *Naganuma Force* shells the airfield throughout the day with heavy artillery.

7. 18 MARCH: 99th Brigade and a squadron of tanks from 9th (Royal Deccan) Horse are ordered to sweep the villages of Kandaingbauk and Shawbyugan. The force runs into heavy opposition from well-placed field and anti-tank guns and loses four tanks.

4. 15 MARCH: During the night two battalions from *55th Infantry Regiment* take up positions around the northwest and eastern sides of the airfield.

5. 16 MARCH: Troops from 99th Indian Infantry Brigade with tanks from 5th (Probyn's) Horse sweep the airfield area and push up the Mandalay road, forcing the Japanese to withdraw.

12. 25–26 MARCH: 48th Brigade with tanks from 5th (Probyn's) Horse and 9th (Royal Deccan) Horse clear the area northeast of Kyigon and push up the Mandalay road, destroying guns and clearing up pockets of Japanese troops.

1. 14 MARCH: During the night one company from *55th Infantry Regiment* and one company from *Mori Special Force* probe the defenses around Meiktila airfield from the northeast and the south.

10. 21–22 MARCH: Countering a build-up by *49th Division* southeast of Meiktila, 99th Brigade runs into stiff resistance around Tamongan.

MAHLAING

MEIKTILA LAKE (NORTH)

MYINDAWGAN LAKE

PINDALE

SHAWBYUGAN

KANDAINGBAUK

KYIGON

KHANDA

AIRFIELD

MANDALAY

MEIKTILA AIRFIELD

THAZI

GBINTHA

NAKA

18th

JAPANESE
A Naganuma Force
B *18th Division*
C 55th Infantry Regiment
D Mori Special Force
E 119th Infantry Regiment
F 14th Tank Regiment
G *49th Division*
H 106th Infantry Regiment
I 168th Infantry Regiment

BRITISH AND INDIAN
1 17th Indian Division HQ and divisional artillery
2 17th Indian Division divisional infantry
3 48th Indian Infantry Brigade
4 63rd Indian Infantry Brigade
5 99th Indian Infantry Brigade
6 9th Indian Infantry Brigade, 5th Indian Division
7 255th Indian Tank Brigade
8 5th (Probyn's) Horse
9 9th (Royal Deccan) Horse

THE DEFENCE OF MEIKTILA
15–29 March 1945, viewed from the southeast, showing the attacks by *18th Division* and *49th Division* on Meiktila Airfield and the town, and 17th Division's active defense, which included a series of aggressive fighting patrols and sorties.

over the *119th Infantry Regiment* and the *Sakuma Force* to boost its strength. These moves were to take effect on 18 March. At the same time, he ordered *28th Army* to make every effort to drive in the bridgehead at Nyaungu. General Honda moved *33rd Army*'s headquarters to a village east of Thazi to be closer to the battle. Despite General Kimura's admonition that Honda co-ordinate the attacks by *18th Division* and *49th Division*, cooperation between the two divisions remained poor throughout the battle for Meiktila. While *18th Division* maintained good radio links with *33rd Army*, amazingly the Division was never able to establish direct radio contact with *49th Division*. Thus all messages from *18th Division* to *49th Division* had to go through *33rd Army*, which itself had trouble getting through to *49th Division*.

In the second half of March the weight of fighting shifted to the eastern sector around Meiktila as both *18th Division* and *49th Division* battled for control over Meiktila's main airfield. *18th Division* concentrated in the area east of the Meiktila–Pindale road between Meiktila's north lake and Myindawgan Lake, where the heavy guns of the *Naganuma Force* could shell the airfield, and the infantry could attack the airfield from the north. *49th Division* concentrated in the villages in and around Nyaungbintha astride the road to Thazi and just south of the airfield. Cowan kept up a vigorous defense, sending out his tank and infantry sweeps to wherever the Japanese could be found, never giving them a chance to build up their forces. Armored car and infantry patrols continued without letup around the main approaches to the town, searching for Japanese positions. RAF Hurricane and Thunderbolt squadrons now joined the Air Commando fighter squadrons in flying cab rank patrols over the battlefield, on call to the VCP teams traveling with the tank and infantry forces. While air strikes caused far

fewer casualties than the dreaded tanks, Allied air superiority around Meiktila proved to be a constant strain on the Japanese. The fighter patrols overhead forced the Japanese soldiers to take every possible precaution not to be discovered, and to spend countless hours digging shelters. The threat of air attack made any movement by day perilous, forcing the Japanese to move mostly by night, restricting their ability to respond to the British sweeps with equivalent force.

The battle for Meiktila's airfield began on the night of 14 March when a company of infantry from the *55th Infantry Regiment* probed the airfield and 99th Brigade's defensive box nearby from the northeast, while at the same time a company from the *Mori Special Force*, a composite battalion formed from men of different units, probed the airfield from the south. Both these forces were driven off, but the next morning the 75mm, 105mm, and 155mm guns of the *Naganuma Force* began shelling the airfield, and kept up a sporadic shelling throughout the day. 15 March was the day that Slim had chosen to fly in 9th Indian Infantry Brigade. The Air Commando C-47s carrying the 9th Brigade landed amid bursts of artillery shells, hurriedly disembarked their troops, and took off again to bring back another load. The airlift continued throughout the day with only a short interruption due to the Japanese shelling. Even with the reinforcements from 9th Brigade, at that time Cowan did not have enough troops to establish a firm perimeter around the airfield. The Japanese were quick to take advantage of this. During the night of 15 March, two battalions from the *55th Infantry Regiment* took up positions around the northwest corner of the airfield and along the eastern side of the field. The following morning a patrol from No. 2708 Field Squadron, RAF Regiment, which had flown into Meiktila on 6 March, uncovered one of these positions and killed 20 Japanese. The airlift of 9th Brigade had to be halted until the Japanese could be cleared from the field. During the day troops from 99th Brigade, with a squadron of tanks from 5th (Probyn's) Horse, swept the airfield and the area up to the Mandalay road, forcing the Japanese to

The aftermath of *49th Division*'s attack on Meiktila during the night of 22/23 March 1945. The *106th Infantry Regiment* lost nearly 200 men in the attack. (IWM IND 4592)

withdraw and destroying two 37mm anti-tank guns and a 75mm gun, and inflicting over 100 casualties. Clearing the airfield now became a daily necessity, but as the Japanese built up their forces around the airfield, the task took longer and longer, steadily reducing the number of hours available to fly in troops and supplies. Now with the airfield under steady artillery fire throughout the day, on 18 March Cowan ordered all landings to be suspended and 17th Division fell back on airdrops for supplies.

While focused on the Japanese concentrations north and south of the airfield, Cowan did not neglect the other approaches to Meiktila. On 17 March he sent two battalions from 63rd Brigade with two squadrons from 5th (Probyn's) Horse on a broad sweep up the Mahlaing road as far as Seywa, then back east toward the Pindale road. In two days of fighting this force cleared several villages and destroyed a number of 47mm anti-tank guns and one 105mm gun. The second day's attacks, on 18 March, were coordinated with a sweep by 99th Brigade and a squadron from 9th (Royal Deccan) Horse. Cowan had ordered 9th Brigade to take over the defense of the airfield, freeing up 99th Brigade for a more offensive role. The Brigade was ordered to clear the villages of Kandaingbauk and Shawbyugan, in between the Pindale and Mandalay roads. Expecting tank sweeps in this area, *18th Division* had brought up three 75mm field artillery pieces and three 75mm mountain guns to use against the tanks, as well as 37mm and 47mm anti-tank guns. The Division sent in the attached *119th Infantry Regiment* to support the *55th Infantry Regiment* covering the area. In the early afternoon the 1st Sikh Light Infantry attacked Kandaingbauk but ran into very heavy artillery and machine-gun fire. The Sikhs were forced back with heavy casualties. The tanks were ordered to move around and attack Shawbyugan from the north, but as they approached the village the anti-tank guns opened up hitting one tank, which immediately brewed up. Moving through the village two tanks from the Squadron HQ troop were also hit and destroyed, while a fourth tank became stuck in a *nullah* and had to be abandoned. Unable to make progress, the force withdrew. *18th Division* then decided to launch a major attack against the airfield during the night of 20 March. The *119th Infantry Regiment* moved into position just east of the

airfield during the night of the 19th, but British tank and infantry sweeps forced them to withdraw the next day. The *55th Infantry Regiment*, with some of *14th Tank Regiment*'s few remaining tanks, tried to break through 99th Brigade's defense box around Kyigon, but heavy artillery and mortar fire broke up the attack.

With *18th Division* hammering at the airfield, Cowan now had to deal with *49th Division* pushing up from the south. *Burma Area Army* had ordered *18th Division* and *49th Division* to make a coordinated attack against Meiktila. Fortunately for 17th Division, their attacks went in independently several days apart, due to the lack of direct communication between the two divisions. Assuming, incorrectly, that *18th Division* had already captured the airfield, 49th *Division's* troops were arrayed in an arc around the southeastern approaches to Meiktila for an attack on the town. A battalion from the *106th Infantry Regiment* moved up to Tamongan, while the Regiment's two other battalions occupied the villages around Kinlu. The Division's cavalry and mountain artillery regiments, with one battalion from the *168th Infantry Regiment*, occupied Kandaung. Once in position these forces began to move forward toward Meiktila. As it became apparent that the Japanese were building up to the southeast, Cowan reacted promptly, sending 9th Brigade with tanks to clear the villages around Nyaungbintha to the east, and 48th Brigade toward Kinlu on 20 March. Neither sweep encountered much resistance, but the next day 48th Brigade with 9th (Royal Deccan) Horse ran into strong Japanese positions in Shwepadaing, west of Kandaung. Despite air strikes and artillery fire, the infantry and tanks made little progress. The Brigade returned to the attack on the 22nd, beginning with a heavy air strike and artillery preparation. In heavy fighting throughout the day the Brigade captured four guns and inflicted more than 100 casualties, but still could not completely clear the villages in the area. To the east, 99th Brigade ran into well-defended bunkers and heavy sniping while trying to clear the villages around Tamongan. That night *49th Division* put in a major attack against Meiktila, with the largest force employed yet. The *106th Infantry Regiment* sent two battalions with over 500 men to attack 48th Brigade's

An Indian infantryman runs past a dead Japanese soldier as he dodges snipers during the fighting at Yewe. (IWM IND 4582)

defensive box. With tremendous effort and heedless of the casualties, the Japanese pushed two 75mm mountain guns right up to the perimeter wire, but artillery and machine-gun fire broke up the attack, which continued throughout the night. The next morning, 48th Brigade found some 200 bodies around the perimeter wire. In the hope of catching the retreating battalions, 63rd Brigade with two squadrons from 5th (Probyn's) Horse attacked Kinde, where they ran into strong opposition from guns and snipers, losing two tanks to hollow-charge shells. The Brigade tried to clear the villages again the next day, but again ran into very heavy fire, 5th (Probyn's) Horse losing a third tank to a hollow-charge shell.

In four days of fighting *49th Division* suffered heavily. The *106th Infantry Regiment* was particularly hard hit and had to withdraw from the battle. With its main striking force spent, the Division was in no position to launch further attacks. This allowed Cowan to bring 63rd Brigade back to Meiktila to join his other brigades in an all-out attempt to clear the airfield, where the Japanese had kept up their attacks by night, and drive the Japanese artillery from their positions northeast of the town. During the night of 24 March, a force of infantry supported by several tanks and artillery attacked 9th Brigade's perimeter near the airfield. The attack was beaten back with artillery and machine-gun fire, but daylight revealed a platoon dug in within one of the aircraft bays on the airfield with an anti-tank gun that opened fire as soon as there was light. Cowan ordered 48th Brigade to sweep up the Mandalay road and clear the area west of the airfield. The Brigade set out on the morning of 25 March with a squadron of tanks from 5th (Probyn's) Horse. The force ran into heavy artillery and machine-gun fire from villages around Kyigon, pinning down the infantry. The tanks moved forward and methodically went after the guns, destroying a 47mm anti-tank gun, one 70mm and one 75mm gun, three machine-guns, and two mortars. The next day it was 9th (Royal Deccan) Horse's turn to work with 48th Brigade, attacking the same area. The Brigade called in air strikes from the cab rank patrol and a heavy artillery bombardment on the area where the Japanese had dug in. As the attack began in the early afternoon the Japanese responded with heavy artillery and mortar fire. The tanks

Rifleman Birkhalai Gurung, 19th Division, firing on Japanese snipers in the ruins of Mandalay. (IWM IND 4533)

A tank commander of 5th (Probyn's) Horse in the turret of his Sherman tank. (IWM IND 4639)

advanced and knocked out two 75mm guns, and then found a 47mm anti-tank gun that was also knocked out without loss. Between the tanks, infantry, and the air and artillery strikes, the Japanese lost over 100 men killed.

For the next three days 48th Brigade and 9th (Royal Deccan) Horse, with additional troops from 9th Brigade, continued to work over the area up to the Mandalay road. The tanks found and destroyed four 70mm and one 75mm field pieces, and a 37mm anti-tank gun, while the infantry flushed out small parties of Japanese troops in the face of heavy small arms fire. By the end of the third day, however, the infantry patrols were reporting more and more villages clear of Japanese troops. While 48th Brigade was clearing the area around the airfield, Cowan ordered 63rd Brigade and 99th Brigade to sweep the area south of Myindawgan Lake, where the heavy artillery of the *Naganuma Force* had been dug in. For several days 99th Brigade had been probing the area north of a sluice that ran into Meiktila Lake north of the town but, in the face of heavy machine-gun fire, could make little progress without tanks, which had difficulty moving over the broken ground. Cowan decided to have 99th Brigade continue to push forward north of the sluice, while 63rd Brigade with tanks from 5th (Probyn's) Horse swept the area between the Mahlaing and Pindale roads and then pushed south to join up with 99th Brigade. On the morning of 27 March the tanks headed west out of Meiktila, and then crossed the Mahlaing road to sweep the area north and south of Myindawgan Lake, hunting for Japanese artillery positions. The tanks found and destroyed a Japanese tank and uncovered a number of ammunition dumps, but found few guns. The tanks went out again the next day to destroy the dumps they had found, and in addition destroyed one 75mm gun and captured a 105mm gun. That same day 63rd Brigade advanced east from the north bank of Meiktila Lake toward the Pindale road while 99th Brigade, following an air strike, tried to move north of the sluice but were again held up by heavy machine-gun fire from bunkers. 63rd Brigade had a more successful day, knocking out six machine-guns and killing over 100 Japanese troops. The next day, against only light opposition, 63rd Brigade turned south and linked up with 99th Brigade north of the sluice.

This effectively marked the end of the battle for Meiktila. After the assaults on the airfield and the town had ended in failure, General Honda, *33rd Army* commander, realized that his two shattered divisions could no longer continue the fight. *18th Division* had lost a third of its strength and half its guns, while *49th Division* had faired even worse, losing nearly two-thirds of its troops and almost all its artillery. To the north, *15th Army* was in full retreat. Mandalay had fallen to 19th Division on 20 March, which then pushed east to Maymyo. XXXIII Corps' other two divisions had both broken out of their bridgeheads in early March. 20th Division went south, sending a strong armored column to capture *18th Division's* administrative headquarters at Wundwin (on the Mandalay–Meiktila road) on 21 March, just as the *Division* was mounting its heaviest attacks on Meiktila airfield. 20th Division then moved east to capture Kyaukse, a *Burma Area Army* supply center. Crossing the Irrawaddy near Ava in between Mandalay and 20th Division's bridgehead, 2nd Division extended its own bridgehead to link up with 20th Division. It then thrust east to capture Ava and join up with 19th Division. While XXXIII Corps was clearing the Irrawaddy bend, IV Corps fought to expand the bridgehead at Nyaungu and re-open the road to Meiktila. Reinforced with a brigade from 5th Division, 7th Division held off repeated attacks on its bridgehead, and then captured Taungtha. By the end of March, 7th Division's units had cleared the road to Meiktila. On 28 March, with IV Corps advancing from the northwest and XXXIII Corps from the north, General Kimura ordered *33rd Army* to abandon the offensive against Meiktila and withdraw to the south, where he hoped the remnants of his broken armies could make a stand. When Cowan's brigades sent out their patrols on 30 March, they found the villages around the airfield and to the south of Meiktila clear of Japanese troops, who had withdrawn the previous night.

In the *Art of War*, Sun Tzu says, "In general, in battle one engages in the orthodox and gains victory through the unorthodox." This is as good a description of the battle for the Irrawaddy bend as any. General Kimura expected the orthodox – an attack on Mandalay. Slim gave Kimura what he expected, but then took advantage of his opponent's expectations to outmaneuver him with the unexpected attack on Meiktila. In using the unorthodox with the orthodox, Slim forced Kimura to bend to his will and fight the battle that Slim wanted to fight. Slim was willing to make the gamble for Meiktila. He had control of the air, a battle-hardened division with a tough, experienced commander, and two aggressive Indian cavalry regiments to lead the attack. All the units involved in the fighting for Meiktila entirely vindicated their commander's faith in them.

AFTERMATH

The re-conquest of Burma now entered its final phase. General Kimura had lost the battle for central Burma, but he still had hopes that his severely depleted forces could stabilize the situation and hold the British advance into southern Burma along a line from Toungoo to Prome. If they could hold on until the monsoon rains inundated Slim's airfields and made the roads to the south impassable, he hoped to achieve a stalemate. Kimura needed to block the main routes to the south and gain time to strengthen his forces, but had precious few resources left to mount a defense. *Burma Area Army* had used up its last reserves in the fighting for Meiktila; it could now only resort to assembling ad-hoc units from administrative and line of communications troops. The rest of Kimura's remaining divisions were now at half strength or less, and all had lost most of their artillery and trucks. Some units were down to a few battalion guns, and there would be no replacements. *15th Army* was a shattered force, its scattered units retreating east into the Shan hills. Kimura ordered all *15th Army* units to retreat and concentrate around Toungoo, where he hoped to reconstitute the remnants back into a fighting force. Responsibility for blocking the main route south fell to General Honda and *33rd Army*, who were ordered to take up defensive positions around Pyawbwe, which lay at the entrance to the Sittang River valley, 25 miles southeast of Meiktila astride the main road and railway line to Rangoon. *33rd Army* was to hold Pyawbwe to cover *15th Army's* retreat, and then withdraw to Toungoo to link up again with *15th Army* and hold a defensive line around Toungoo. After their mauling at Meiktila, the combined strength of *33rd Army's* *18th*, *49th*, and *53rd Divisions* made up less than half a full division, far from adequate for the job *33rd Army* had been given. To the west, Kimura assigned *28th Army* the task of blocking the approaches to Rangoon down the Irrawaddy River valley and holding a defensive line around Prome. General Sakurai was to hold the British forces north of Prome to give him time to withdraw his *54th Division* from the Arakan front as reinforcements. If Kimura could hold southern Burma until the monsoon, he could delay any British offensive south toward Malaya or east into Thailand.

Where Kimura looked to the approaching monsoon for relief, General Slim viewed it with

A Stuart tank of the 7th Light Cavalry on the road to Rangoon. (IWM IND 4652)

Sherman tanks of the 9th (Royal Deccan) Horse and 17th Division infantry attacking Pyinbongyi, 60 miles north of Rangoon at the end of April 1945. (IWM IND 4650)

mounting anxiety. When the monsoon began in early May, the torrential rains would play havoc with 14th Army's lines of communications back to India, which were already stretched to the limit. Slim fully expected the Japanese to defend Rangoon with the same tenacity they had demonstrated at Meiktila. The thought of his army bogged down in house-to-house fighting around Rangoon, in the monsoon, with its supply lines in disarray, and the threat of the withdrawal of the American air transport squadrons around 1 June, was a nightmare. To ease the burden on the supply system, Slim decided to withdraw his two British infantry divisions, 2nd Division and 36th Division, which were short of British troops, and rely on his five Indian infantry divisions for the last stage of the battle. He planned to advance on Rangoon along two axes, with one corps moving down the road and rail corridor that stretched from Mandalay to Rangoon following the Sittang River, and his second corps advancing down both banks of the Irrawaddy River. Once again speed was vital to 14th Army's success. Slim knew that as his divisions left the more open country in the central plains and pushed deeper into the wetter Irrawaddy delta region, they would become more dependent on roads and the bridges that crossed the many small rivers and *chaungs* that fed the Irrawaddy and the Sittang rivers. He could not afford to give the Japanese time to consolidate and prepare strong defenses around the key bridges along the route south. He assigned the task of pushing down the road and rail corridor to General Messervy and IV Corps and gave the Irrawaddy River route to Stopford and XXXIII Corps, but re-allocated his divisions amongst the two corps. Slim gave 14th Army's two mechanized divisions, 5th Division and 17th Division, to IV Corps, as they were best equipped to move with speed. The two divisions would leapfrog one another on the way to Rangoon, with one division speeding ahead while the other stopped to deal with any resistance encountered. Slim gave 19th Division back to IV Corps to guard the Mandalay–Meiktila area and IV Corps' rear areas. Since 7th Division was already in position along the Irrawaddy, it joined XXXIII Corps to advance down the west bank of the Irrawaddy, while 20th Division crossed over from the Mandalay area to advance down the east bank. Slim's two armored brigades remained with their respective corps. Still concerned by the possibility of delay, Slim asked Mountbatten to resurrect Operation "Dracula" in a modified form – a sea-borne invasion of Rangoon by one division from the Arakan to be scheduled for the first week of May. If both his two corps got bogged down, "Dracula" would provide insurance.

Slim wasted no time. He had already given his commanders operational instructions for the advance to Rangoon on 18 March, even before the battle for Meiktila was over. After the capture of the town, No. 221 Group moved its fighter wings to the captured airfields around Meiktila to remain within range of 14th Army's advance. With the briefest of pauses IV Corps started south. The Corps' first objective was to smash through *33rd Army's* positions around Pyawbwe to gain access to the main road to Rangoon. Messervy assigned the task to 17th Division and 255th Tank Brigade. After meeting stubborn resistance around Yindaw, Cowan planned an envelopment of Pyawbwe using his full strength, with 48th Brigade attacking from the north, 63rd Brigade from the west, and 99th Brigade from the east, while an armored column from 255th Tank Brigade drove past the town and came up from the south. In three days of fierce fighting 17th Division tore *33rd Army* apart. When the town fell on 10 April, Cowan's troops counted over 1,000 dead. The remnants of Honda's three divisions retreated east into the hills. In one of the few tank-versus-tank actions of the campaign, the Shermans of 5th (Probyn's) Horse destroyed the last remaining tanks of the *14th Tank Regiment*. Leaving 17th Division behind to mop up, 5th Division then raced ahead, capturing Toungoo on 22 April. The speed of the advance caught several Japanese columns by surprise, and on a few occasions 5th Division's advanced units managed to capture vital bridges before the Japanese were aware of the British presence. To the west, XXXIII Corps had cleared the area west of Meiktila then began its drive down the Irrawaddy, capturing Chauk on 18 April and the vital oilfields around Yenangyaung on 26 April. In these last weeks of fighting the Japanese Army Air Force made a final, though futile, effort to support *Burma Area Army*. The *64th Sentai* sent flights of eight to ten "Oscar" fighters on sweeps against Messervy's advancing columns on four occasions, destroying a number of vehicles and five gliders on an advance airfield and causing a number of casualties, but failing to slow the advance. After flying its last mission on 29 April, the *64th Sentai* withdrew to Thailand to join the rest of the *4th Hikodan*.

At Toungoo 17th Division took over the advance from 5th Division, and headed south for Pegu, some 50 miles from Rangoon. When the Division reached Pegu on the morning of 29 April, the Japanese commander blew the bridges across the Pegu River and put up a spirited defense that delayed the capture of the town. That night the monsoon broke ... two weeks early. Cowan's troops cleared the town, but although engineers managed to get a Bailey bridge across the Pegu River, torrential rains flooded the approaches to the bridge, preventing a crossing. The rains caught XXXIII Corps approaching Prome, a long way from Rangoon. It was galling to come up short having come so far. Fortunately, however, the capture of Rangoon proved to be somewhat of an anti-climax – the Japanese had withdrawn. Kimura had chosen not to defend the city and, following a paratroop assault and an air strike on Japanese positions at the entrance to the mouth of the Irrawaddy on 1 May, the "Dracula" naval force launched troops of 26th Division in the early hours of 2 May who made an unopposed landing south of Rangoon. The next day,

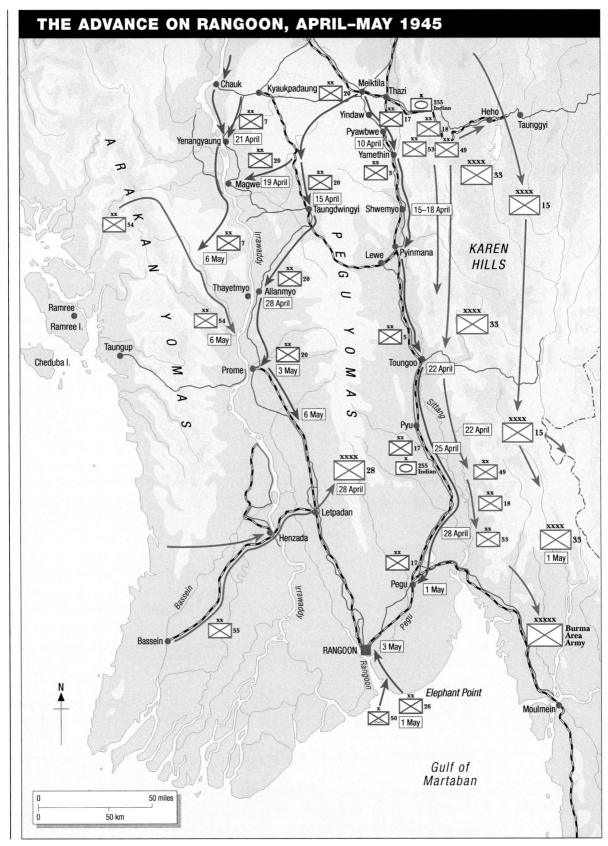

26th Division sent launches up the river to the city to be met by an RAF wing commander who, seeing no sign of the Japanese in Rangoon, had landed his Mosquito at Mingaladon the day before.

The campaign to re-conquer Burma was over, although the fighting continued up to the surrender on 15 August 1945, as the remnants of *15th Army* and *33rd Army* struggled to hold open a route for the troops of *28th Army* to escape across the Pegu Yomas and into the hills of eastern Burma. In the fighting from the capture of Rangoon to the surrender, *Burma Area Army* lost nearly as many men as it had in the battles around Mandalay and Meiktila. In a little less than a year, 14th Army had marched and fought its way from Imphal to Rangoon, never giving *Burma Area Army* a chance to regain the initiative, and smashing its divisions between the hammer around Mandalay and the anvil at Meiktila.

THE BATTLEFIELD TODAY

There are few signs evident today of the storm that swept over Nyaungu and Meiktila during February and March of 1945. Burma, now known as Myanmar, is a bit off the beaten track of usual tourist destinations, but is not that difficult to visit by oneself or as part of a package tour. The military government that rules Myanmar is trying to encourage tourism, and has made steps to improve tourist facilities and services. Today it is relatively easy to visit both Nyaungu and Meiktila.

Nyaungu is the entry point for a visit to Myanmar's ancient capital at Pagan, a few miles away. There are daily flights from Yangon (formerly Rangoon) to Nyaungu, and now there is a wide range of accommodations from simple guesthouses to full-service hotels. The town of Nyaungu itself has grown to accommodate the increasing number of foreign tourists, and bears little resemblance to the smaller village that existed there in 1945. Since 14th Army passed through Nyaungu relatively quickly and without much activity, the town itself is of less interest than the landing beaches to the east, which have remained more or less the same as they were in February 1945. The land to the east of the town is dry and uncultivated, and as a consequence has not been built up. There is a dirt road just to the east of the town center that leads to the temples atop 'B4', 'B3', and 'B2' beaches about a mile away. Passable in the dry season with a car, this road might be more difficult during the monsoon season. From Kondaw-gyi temple, the highest point behind the beaches, one can look out across the Irrawaddy River to B beach on the other side. The river has changed its course over the years, and a large sand bar now sits where there was a clear

A modern view of "B4" Beach (center) with "B3" Beach to the right, remarkably unchanged since 1945. The 4/15th Punjab Regiment landed here on the morning of 14 February. (Author's collection)

One of the few remaining buildings in Meiktila from the period of the battle. The former home and office of a money lender, the building still shows scars of the fighting in early March. (Author's collection)

channel in 1945. At the ferry landing at Nyaungu one can hire a small boat and ask the owner to go up the river to look at the landing beaches as they would have appeared to the 6/15th Punjab soldiers on the morning of 14 February. While there are more trees around the beaches today than in 1945, the vista is strikingly similar to photographs of the landing beaches taken that day.

With a car and driver one can get to Meiktila from Nyaungu in about four hours, following roughly the same route 17th Division took through Welaung, Taungtha, and Mahlaing. Meiktila itself has changed almost beyond recognition. The population of the town has expanded five-fold from the roughly 30,000 people that lived in and around the town in 1945. The town today is a busy district center with several military bases around the outskirts. About all that remains from the wartime period is the street layout and a few of the temples at the north end of town and around Point 860. The areas around the town that were open fields in 1945 are now residential neighborhoods. A severe fire in the early 1990s destroyed much of the center of the town, including many of the older buildings. Others have been torn down and rebuilt over time with more modern multi-story structures and rows of two and three-story shops. There are a few buildings left from the war, but one has to hunt them out. Still, one can follow the main roads into the town and trace the path 48th Brigade took as it fought its way into Meiktila from the north and northeast, and circle the broken ground below the temple at Point 860 where 5th (Probyn's) Horse and 9th (Royal Deccan) Horse fought to clear the Japanese bunkers in the area. About 100 meters past the causeway across Meiktila Lake, in the western part of town, there is the small Nagayon Temple that holds the remains of a Japanese Type 95 *Ha-Go* light tank. This tank served with the *14th Tank Regiment* in the battle. It is one of the very few visible signs that a battle was ever fought here. Japanese veteran associations have built a memorial in the temple grounds to those who died during the fighting. A wooden cabinet in the temple holds a British and a Japanese helmet, some bayonets, and a rusted and dirt-encrusted Nambu pistol. It is best to visit the town in late February or early March, when one can experience the heat and the thirst that comes with the hot season, and think back on the soldiers of both armies who fought courageously for a town that now barely remembers them.

SELECT BIBLIOGRAPHY

Allen, Louis, *Burma: The Longest War*, J.M. Dent & Sons Ltd. (London, 1984)

Brett-James, Anthony, *Ball of Fire: The Fifth Indian Division in the Second World War*, Gale & Polden Ltd. (Aldershot, 1951)

Drea, Edward J., *In The Service of the Emperor: Essays on the Imperial Japanese Army*, University of Nebraska Press (Lincoln, 1998)

Evans, Lieutenant-General Sir Geoffrey, *Slim As Military Commander*, B.T. Batsford Ltd. (London, 1969)

— —, *The Desert And The Jungle*, William Kimber (London, 1959)

Farndale, Major-General Sir Martin, *History of the Royal Artillery Regiment: The Far East Theatre 1941–46*, Brassey's (London, 2002)

Fraser, George MacDonald, *Quartered Safe Out Here: A Recollection of the War in Burma*, Harvill (London, 1992)

Gilmore, Scott, *A Connecticut Yankee in the 8th Gurkha Rifles: A Burma Memoir*, Brassey's (London, 1995)

Hill, John, *China Dragons: A Rifle Company at War, Burma 1944–45*, Blandford (London, 1991)

Khera, P.N. and Prasad, S.N., *Official History of the Indian Armed Forces in the Second World War 1939–45: The Reconquest of Burma, Volume II*, Combined Inter-Services Historical Section (Delhi, 1959)

Kirby, Major-General S. Woodburn, *The War Against Japan, Volume IV: The Reconquest of Burma*, HMSO (London, 1965)

Perrett, Bryan, *Tank Tracks to Rangoon: The Story of British Armour in Burma*, Robert Hale Ltd. (London, 1978)

Probert, Air Commodore Henry, *The Forgotten Air Force: The Royal Air Force in the War Against Japan 1941–1945*, Brassey's (London, 1995)

Roberts, Brigadier M.R., *Golden Arrow: The Story of the 7th Indian Division*, Gale & Polden Ltd. (Aldershot, 1952)

Slim, Field Marshal Sir William, *Defeat Into Victory*, Cassell (London, 1956)

Smeeton, Miles, *A Change of Jungles*, Rupert Hart-Davies (London, 1962)

Young, Edward, *Air Commando Fighters of World War II*, Specialty Press (North Branch, 2000)

INDEX

Figures in **bold** refer to illustrations

14th Army (British and Commonwealth)
  24th Indian Mountain Artillery regiment
    28
  36th Infantry Division 12, 88
  116th Tank Regiment **48**
  commanders 8, 17–19
  Japanese expectations of actions 21–2
  Operation "Capital" 11, 12–13
  Operation "U-Go" 10
  order of battle 32
  qualities and doctrine 28–9
  strategy 8, 9, 11, 22–3
  weapons 29–31
14th Army: 5th Indian Infantry Division **7, 20**
  9th Infantry Brigade 68, 78–9, 81
  and Imphal 7, 19
  and Rangoon 88, 89
14th Army: IV Corps
  1st Air Commando Group 30, 31, 43, 48,
    50–2, 56, 65
  2nd Air Commando Group 31, 65
  19th Indian Infantry Division 12
  commanders 19
  and Irrawaddy 13, 23, 35–7, **38**, 40–5, **50–2**
  and Meiktila 46–86, **54**
  objectives 23
  and Rangoon 88–9
14th Army: IV Corps: 7th Indian Infantry
  Division
  2nd South Lancs Regiment 42–3, 44,
    47–9, **49**, **50–2**
  33rd Brigade 41, 42–3, 44, 46, 48–9, **50–2**
  89th Brigade 41, 42–3, 46, 48–9
  114th Brigade 40–1, 42–3, 44, 46–7
  and Irrawaddy 36, 37, 40–4, **41–3**, 47–8,
    47–9, **50–2**
  and Meiktila 47–68, 86
  and Rangoon (as part of XXIII Corps) 88
14th Army: IV Corps: 17th Indian Infantry
  Division **72**
  5th (Probyn's) Horse, and attack on
    Meiktila 53, 54–5, **55**, 56–7, **56**, 58, 61,
    65, 66
  5th (Probyn's) Horse, and defense of
    Meiktila 71, 73, 78–9, 81–2, 83, 84, 85, **85**
  9th Brigade **80**, 81, 82, 83, 84, 85
  9th (Royal Deccan) Horse, and attack on
    Meiktila 53, 54, 56, 58–9, 60, 61, 64, 65,
    66–7
  9th (Royal Deccan) Horse, and defense of
    Meiktila 72, 73–7, 78–9, 82, 83, 84–5
  9th (Royal Deccan) Horse, and Rangoon,
    88
  11th Cavalry (P.A.V.O.) 71–2
  48th Brigade, and attack on Meiktila 45,
    53–7, 60, **62–64**, 65, 66–7
  48th Brigade, and defense of Meiktila 69,
    72, 73–7, 78–9, 83–5
  48th Brigade, and Rangoon, 89
  59th Field Battery **48**

63rd Brigade, and attack on Meiktila 45,
    53, 56, 58–9, 60, 65, 66, 67
  63rd Brigade, and defense of Meiktila 69,
    72–3, 76, 78–9, 82, 84, 85
  63rd Brigade, and Rangoon 89
  99th Brigade, and attack on Meiktila 45,
    53, 56, **57**
  99th Brigade, and defense of Meiktila 69,
    78–9, 81–3, 85
  99th Brigade, and Rangoon 89
  and Irrawaddy 36, 44, 46, 49
  and Meiktila 53–7, **53**, 60–8, **61**, 69–85
  and Rangoon 88, 89
  reorganization into motorized division
    44–5
  "Tomcol" 49, 54
14th Army: IV Corps: 28th East African
  Brigade 23, 36, 37, 40–1, 44, 46
14th Army: IV Corps: 255th Indian Tank
  Brigade
  16th Cavalry 36, 60, 71, **72**
  background 30, 36
  and Irrawaddy 42–3, 46
  and Meiktila 53, 54, 56, 58–9, 60, 64, 65,
    67, 69
  and Rangoon 89
14th Army: IV Corps: Lushai Brigade 23,
  36–7, **36**
14th Army: XXIII Corps
  and Chindwin 12
  commanders 19
  and Irrawaddy 13, 33–5, 37–40, **38**, 45
  objectives 22–3
  and Rangoon 88, 89–91
14th Army: XXIII Corps: 2nd Division **7, 37**
  and Imphal 7
  and Irrawaddy 48
  and Mandalay 68, 77, **77**, 86
  and Shwebo 33, 35, 37
  withdrawn 88
14th Army: XXIII Corps: 19th Indian
  Infantry Division **39**
  and Mandalay 39–40, 45, 46, 68, 77, 85
  and Rangoon (as part of IV Corps) 88
  and Shwebo 33, 35, 37
14th Army: XXIII Corps: 20th Indian
  Infantry Division
  and Mandalay 45, 47, **47**, 68
  and Monywa 33, 35, 37, 39, **39**, **40**
  move south 85–6
  and Rangoon 88, 89–91
14th Army: XXIII Corps: 254th Indian Tank
  Brigade 23, 30, 35, 45
14th Army: XXIII Corps: 268th Indian
  Infantry Brigade 23, 33–5

air power and campaigns 31
  "Earthquake" bombardment mission 36–7
  and Irrawaddy 43, 48, **50–2**, 53
  and Meiktila 56, 65, 71, 80–1, 84
  Monywa bombardment 37–9
  and supplies 10, 28, 30, 31, 36, 71

Visual Control Point (VCP) jeeps, 31, **57**
  see also Japanese Army Air Force; Royal Air
    Force
aircraft
  C-47 **30, 69, 80**
  Dakota **36**
  Hurricane Mk. IV **22**
  Ki.43 *Hayabusa* fighter **27**
  P-47D **31, 49, 50–2, 65**
  P-51D **31**
  Spitfire **45**
American forces 7–8, 9, 68
  see also US Army Air Force
anti-tank guns 26–7, **26**, 29–30
armored cars **72**
artillery 26–7, 29–30, 69
  see also howitzers
Assam 10, 11
Auchinleck, Gen Sir Claude 28
Ava 86

bomb shelters **73**
British and Commonwealth forces see
  14th Army; Royal Air Force
Burma **6**
  strategic importance 8–9
  terrain 8, **8**, 9, **33**, 35
Burma Area Army (Japanese; part of
  Southern Army) **24**
  24th Independent Mixed Brigade 21
  and Meiktila 57–60, 68–9, 71–86, **81**
  commanders 16–17
  composition, strength and doctrine 20–2,
    24–5
  last days 87, 91
  and Operation "U-Go" 9–10
  order of battle 32
  retreat over Irrawaddy 13
  strategy 9–10, 11–12, 20–2
  weapons 25–7
Burma Area Army: 2nd Division 21
  16th Infantry Regiment 54–5
Burma Area Army: 15th Army
  and British crossing of Irrawaddy 44
  commander replaced 12
  objectives 21
  Operation "U-Go" 10, 20
  reinforcements given to 33rd 69
  retreat 85, 87
Burma Area Army: 15th Army: 15th Division
  21, 40
Burma Area Army: 15th Army: 31st Division
  21, 37
Burma Area Army: 15th Army: 33rd Division
  21, 36, 37, 47, **50–2**
  214th Infantry Regiment 46, 47, 56, 69
  215th Infantry Regiment 47
Burma Area Army: 15th Army: 53rd Division
  21, 40
  119th Infantry Regiment 69
Burma Area Army: 28th Army 21, 44, 80, 87
  72nd Independent Mixed Brigade 21, 46

Burma Area Army: 28th Army: 49th Division 21, 27, 69
  168th Infantry Regiment 60
Burma Area Army: 28th Army: 54th Division 7, 11, 21, 87
Burma Area Army: 28th Army: 55th Division 21
Burma Area Army: 33rd Army 17, 21, 77, 80, 87, 89
Burma Area Army: 33rd Army: 18th Division 21, 27, 68–9, 71–86
  14th Tank Regiment **25**, 26, 69, 78–9, 83, 89
  55th Infantry Regiment 78–9, 81, 82–3
  56th Infantry Regiment 73
  119th Infantry Regiment 78–9, 80, 82–3
  214th Infantry Regiment 69, 72, 73
  Mori Special Force 78–9
  Naganuma Force 69, 78–9, 80, 85
  Sakuma Force 69, 80
Burma Area Army: 33rd Army: 49th Division 21, 27, 69, 72, 80, 83–4, 86
  106th Infantry Regiment 77, 78–9, **81**, 83–4
  168th Infantry Regiment 78–9
Burma Area Army: 33rd Army: 56th Division 21

China 7–8, 9, 10–11, 68
Chindits 9, 10
Chindwin River 12, 33, **35**
Cowan, MajGen D.T. "Punch" **18**, 19
  and Irrawaddy 41, 45, 49
  and Meiktila 53, 60, 65–6, 68, 69–72, 76, 80–5
  and Rangoon 89
  Slim on 66

"Earthquake" bombardment mission 36–7
elephants 41, **41**
Evans, MajGen Geoffrey 19, **19**, 41, 44

Fazal Din, Naik 66

Gangaw 36–7
Gracy, MajGen Douglas 19
Gurung, Birkhalai **85**

Hedley, Brig **66**
Hletaikon 77
Honda Masaki, LtGen **16**, 17, 77, 80, 85
howitzers **21**, **25**, **60**
"Hump" air link 7, 10–11

Imphal, battle of 7, 10
Indian Army 10, 29
  see also individual divisions under 14th Army
Indian National Army 20, 47, 48, 52
Irrawaddy River
  British clearance 77, 85–6
  British crossing 22–3, 33–53, **39**, **40**, **47–9**
  description 41
  Japanese retreat over 13
  Japanese troop dispositions 21
  landing beaches 52, 92–3, **92**
  strategic importance 20

Japanese Army Air Force (JAAF) 27–8, 49–53, 57–60, 89
Japanese land forces see Southern Army

Kaing 56
Kalemyo 12, **12**
Kalewa 12
Kandaingbauk 78–9, 82
Kanhla 46
Kanlebu 37

Kasuya Tomekichi, MajGen 57–60, 67
Katamura Shihachi, LtGen 12, **16**, 17, 39–40, 57, 69, 77
Kawabe Masakazu, LtGen 10, 11–12
Khan, Capt Hassan **11**
Khanda 60–1
Khanna 65, 66
Kimura Hyotaro, LtGen 16, **16**
  appointment 11–12
  and Meiktila 57, 68–9, 77–80, 86
  orders retreat across Irrawaddy 13
  and retreat south 87
  strategy 20–2
Kinde 84
Kinlu 83
Kohima 10
Kyangyagon 73
Kyaukmyaung 39, 40
Kyaukse 86
Kyigon 69, 78–9, 83, 84

Leese, Gen Sir Oliver 17, **17**, 23
Leindaw 73

Mahlaing 53, 56
Mandalay
  Allied plans to capture 10, 11, 12
  British advance and capture 77, **77**, 85, **85**
  British feint towards 22–3, 35, 45, 47
  importance to Japanese 21
Meiktila **93**
  airfield **69**, 78–9, 81–3, 84
  British attack on 46–68, **60**, **61**, **67**
  British defense of 68–86, **70**, **81**
  British strategy 22–3, 44–5
  description 65
  Japanese plans for defense 21–2, 57–60
  nowadays **93**, **93**
Messervy, LtGen Sir Frank 18, **18**
  and Irrawaddy 23, 33, 36–7, 40–5, 46, 49, 52
  and Meiktila 65–6
  and Rangoon 88
Mile Stone 8 56
Mile Stone 319 72
Monywa 35, 37–9, **39**, **40**
Mountbatten, Adm Lord Louis 9, 10–11, 17, **17**, 68, 69
Mutaguchi Renya, LtGen 10, 12
Myindawgan Lake 73, 78–9, 80, 85

Naganuma, Col 69
Ngathayauk 53, 54
Nicholson, MajGen C.G.G. 19
Northern Combat Area Command (N.C.A.C.) 9, 12, 68
Nyaugbintha 80, 83
Nyaungu 41–4, 47, 49, 80, 86, 92–3

"Octagon" Conference (1944) 11
Operation "Capital" 11, 12–13
Operation "Cloak" 44, 46
Operation "Dracula" 11, 89–91, **91**
Operation "Extended Capital" 22–3, 33, **34**
Operation "Ha-Go" 10, 17
Operation "Multivite" 46
Operation "U-Go" 9–10
orders of battle 32
Oyin 54–5

pagodas **35**
Pakokku 36, 44, 46–7
Pauk 46
Pegu 89

Pinlebu 12
Point 860 61, 65
Pyawbwe 87, 89
Pyinbongyi **88**

"Quadrant" Conference (1943) 9

Raidon, Havildar **36**
Rangoon
  Allied plans to capture 10, 11, 33
  fight for 68, 87–91, **90**, **91**
Rees, MajGen "Pete" 12, 19
Royal Air Force (RAF)
  No. 20 Squadron 22
  No. 152 Squadron 53
  No. 221 Group 45, 89
  No. 2708 Field Squadron 81
  support for campaign 31, 37, 45, 53, 80–1
  see also air power and campaigns

Sagaing 45
Sakurai Shozo, LtGen 17, **17**, 87
Seikpyu 44, 46
Seywa **53**, 54
Shawbyugan 78–9, 82
Shwebo and Shwebo plain 12–13, 35, **37**
Shwepadaing 78–9, 83
Singh, Lt Bahadur **55**
Singh, Jemmadar Gopal **11**
Singu 46
Slim, LtGen Sir William 17–18, **17**, **72**
  observations of actions 36–7, 65–6
  strategy and orders, general 8–9, 10–11, 12–13
  strategy and orders, Meiktila 22–3, 33, 35, 36, 41, 45, 68
  strategy and orders, Rangoon 87–9
  and troop morale 9, 28–9
South-East Asia Command, formation 9
Southern Army see Burma Area Army
Stillwell, Gen Joseph 9
Stopford, LtGen Sir Montague 19, 23, 33–5, 45, 88
supplies, British 9, 10, 23, 28, 30, 31, 36

Tamongan 83
tanks
  importance in campaign 30–1
  Model 95 Ha-Go **25**, 26, 93
  Model 97 Chi-Ha 26
  Sherman 26, **29**, **48**, **56**, **73**, 77, **82**, **83**
  Stuart **47**, **87**
Taungtha 53, 56, 86
Terauchi Hiraichi, Field Marshal Count 16
Thabutkon 53, 56, 69
Thangongyi 72
Tiddim 12, **20**
Toungoo 87

US Army Air Force (USAAF) 31, 37, 68
  see also air power and campaigns

Visual Control Point (VCP) jeeps 31, **57**

weapons 25–7, 29–31
Weston, Lt W.B. 67
Wetlet 72–3, **74–76**
Wingate, MajGen Orde 9, 10
Wundwin 85

Yego 72
Yenangyaung oil fields 20, 21, 46
Yeu 37
Yewe **81**, **82**